Journey to Texas, 1833

Journey
— TO —
TEXAS
1833

Detlef Dunt

TRANSLATED FROM THE GERMAN BY
Anders Saustrup

EDITED AND WITH AN INTRODUCTION BY
**James C. Kearney and
Geir Bentzen**

UNIVERSITY OF TEXAS PRESS
Austin

First edition, 2015

Requests for permission to reproduce material
from this work should be sent to:
Permissions
University of Texas Press
P.O. Box 7819
Austin, TX 78713-7819
http://utpress.utexas.edu/index.php/rp-form

The paper used in this book meets the minimum requirements of
ANSI/NISO Z39.48-1992 (R1997) (Permanence of Paper). ∞

Design by Lindsay Starr

LIBRARY OF CONGRESS CATALOGING-IN-PUBLICATION DATA
Dunt, Detlef, author.
[Reise nach Texas. English]
Journey to Texas, 1833 / Detlef Dunt ; translated from the German
by Anders Saustrup ; edited and with an introduction by
James C. Kearney and Geir Bentzen. — First edition.
pages cm
Includes bibliographical references.
ISBN 978-0-292-74021-1 (cloth : alk. paper)
ISBN 978-0-292-76836-9 (library e-book)
ISBN 978-0-292-76837-6 (non-library e-book)
ISBN 978-1-477-31350-3

1. Germans—Texas. 2. Texas—Description and travel. 3. Texas—Emigration
and immigration. I. Saustrup, Anders, 1930–2008, translator.
II. Kearney, James C., 1946–, editor. III. Bentzen, Geir, editor. IV. Title.
F395.G3D86 2015
976.4′03—dc23

2014046919

doi:10.7560/740211

Contents

Journey to Texas, 1833

An Introduction

James C. Kearney and Geir Bentzen

THE STORY OF Detlef Dunt's voyage to Texas in 1833–1834 is much more than a travelogue. First published in Germany after Dunt returned there in 1834, the book is a multigenerational story of paced immigration and settlement, of acquiring land, of organizing a society with institutions, and of giving the ultimate sacrifice for the land and people in the Civil War. It is also the story of the Jordt family in Colorado County, Texas.

We have been working to publish this translation from German to English since 2010. Anders Saustrup made the translation sometime in the 1990s; at least that is what we believe. The typewritten manuscript lingered unpublished in Saustrup's home and was found there by Bill Stein of the Nesbitt Memorial Library in Columbus after Saustrup had passed away in 2008. Stein contacted James C. Kearney about working on the manuscript, but soon after Stein also passed.

THE NAME OF Detlef Dunt is forever connected to this first German book about Texas. The problem with Dunt has always been that we knew little about him, and understood little of what drove him to Texas and back to Germany several times. Dunt read at least one letter by an earlier German settler, Friedrich Ernst, who arrived in present-day Industry in 1832 and wrote letters to friends back home about the opportunities and easy lifestyle awaiting them in Texas. In doing so, Ernst became part of an epistolary pattern that lured settlers across the Atlantic for several decades. Not long after reading Ernst's letter, Dunt decided to go to Texas and see it for himself. How could he do that while planning to return to his homeland? It was entirely too expensive for most people to cross and recross the ocean to inspect the New World. The common immigrant sold what little he and his family owned and made the voyage without any possible return in mind. And Dunt considered himself a common man—a conceit that Saustrup accepted, describing Dunt in this way:

> What [Detlef Dunt] thought and knew in advance about America—a common term abroad for the United States—we do not know.
>
> Detlef Dunt would not have hesitated to call himself a common man, and did so, only using different words. More than just a common man, he was also a common denominator of sorts, representing circumstances shared by many, who, however, did not have his articulate ability to write about them. For latter-day readers, it is felicitous that his book has such qualities rather than being intensely individualistic. To us, he is virtually anonymous as well, so we may say, in the words of Thomas Mann, that we want to tell his story not for his sake, but for the sake of the story. It is his very commonness that makes him so uncommon.[1]

We know more now about Detlef Dunt and his circumstances than was known when Anders Saustrup wrote the text quoted above. Although Saustrup accepts Dunt's self-description, the book and the voyages tell us that Dunt could hardly have been so common after all. He was resourceful, educated, knowledgeable, and a fast and observant learner. He also had enough money to put his life in Germany aside long enough to investigate Ernst's claims before returning to his home and family.

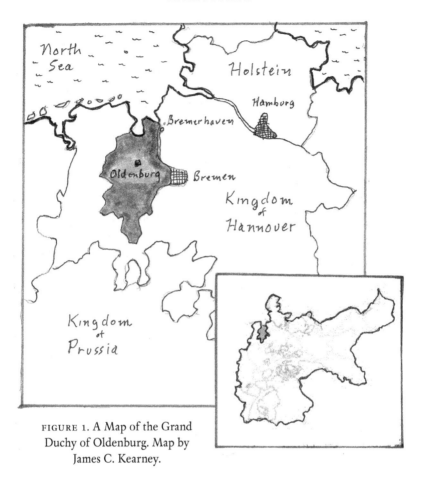

FIGURE 1. A Map of the Grand
Duchy of Oldenburg. Map by
James C. Kearney.

In real life Detlef Dunt was named Detlef Thomas Friedrich
Jordt. He was born in Lütjenburg in eastern Holstein on May 7,
1793.[2] For centuries Holstein had been a divided political landscape dominated by dukes of the Danish royal family. In Jordt's
time the area was united under the Danish king, who also carried the title of Duke of Holstein. This simple arrangement was
a recent development; in earlier times the area had been subdi-
vided among the family members. The languages spoken would
have been Low German dialects related to High German, Dutch,
and Scandinavian languages. Some people may have used Danish
or Swedish. The area is in the far north of present-day Germany

and borders on both the Baltic and the North Sea coasts. Trade had long been a main source of wealth. The ancient trade route from the north went via Haithabu on the east coast across the peninsula to the Atlantic coast and into the English Channel. Trade routes can easily be understood by the old rule: water ties together, land divides. Othere, a Norwegian trader who came all the way from northern Norway to the court of King Alfred of Wessex in the 880s, provided an early report on Haithabu, remarking that he had been to the White Sea in the far north of present Russia and had passed by Haithabu on his way to England. He knew who lived in the area: "[. . .] this stands between the Wends and the Saxons and the Angles, and belongs to the Danes." He also mentioned that the "Angles dwelt in those lands before they came here to this country" [England].[3]

The location is at the narrowest and lowest-lying point of land between the Baltic and the North Sea. In general the area was and still is a meeting place for traders and travelers, a place where two oceans and several large rivers meet and make heavy transportation possible. The opportunities for trade must have been vastly superior to most other areas of Europe. The mental outlook of a person growing up in this area was very different from that of someone from a quiet agricultural area with few strangers and without the commercial activity that characterized Holstein. Traveling far and wide was normal; it was part of the local culture.

Jordt is thought to have been the son of a *Kaufmann*, which in German can mean a store owner or any other sort of businessman, large or small, rich or poor. His father may have been Matthias Jordt, mayor of Lütjenburg from 1785 to 1800. Matthias Jordt had also been the city administrator, and he administered a number of properties around the city owned by nobles. The two Jordt families in the area are both thought to have come from Copenhagen in Denmark. Matthias Jordt was married to Johanna Christiane, born von Dundten. She was the daughter of a Danish officer, Gerhardt Hinrich von Dundten. The name was sometimes shortened to Dundt. Their son got his simplified Detlef Dunt pseudonym from his mother's side. His father died in 1801 and his mother in 1807. Both his father and his maternal grandfather had been Schützenkönig, or rifle shooting champion, in their hometown. The yearly competition and festivities are important social events in Germany to this day. His grandfather won in 1767 and his father in 1785. One of the four sides of a pyramid decoration built for the festivities of 1785 was not in German, but more in Danish: "Wi synge, onßka bröderlich—Gid Himmeln vel singe dig!" (We sing, wish brotherly—May the Heavens bless you!).[4]

Detlef Jordt married Dorothea Heeder, from the duchy of Oldenburg, in 1819.[5] He applied for a permit to settle in the city of Oldenburg in 1827, which he received only after his father-in-law and brother-in-law guaranteed that he would not be a burden to society. The Jordt family already had three children at this time, with their fourth soon to follow. According to historian Walter Struve, the family settled in the Berne/Wesermarsch area (*Wesermarsch* means the marsh or wet bottomland by the river Weser) to be close to the in-laws.

Little is known about this period in Jordt's life. In his book he provides one comment on the area when he describes setting out on his voyage to Texas aboard the bark *Leontine*: "For quite some time we could still see the Oldenburg coastline and the churches of Burhave and Langwarden. I cannot express what feelings overcame me seeing this. I had previously lived for two years in the first-mentioned church village, and so many memories of pleasures enjoyed there, as well as bitter pain, unintentionally became associated with the view of that coast and that church tower."[6]

We know nothing else about his time in Burhave on the North Sea coast northwest of Bremerhaven, but we may speculate a bit about the bitter pain he mentions. In the early 1800s a type of malaria called the cold fever raged in Burhave. The average life expectancy fell to less than thirty years. The town's inhabitants were also forced to work for the French occupiers during the Napoleonic wars. On February 3 and 4, 1825, an enormous storm flood hit the area. The flood marks reached more than seventeen feet above normal sea level. Large areas of land that had been pumped dry and protected by dikes in the years after the large flood of 1717 reverted to wetlands again and much coastal land was lost. By 1826 most land in Holstein had been mortgaged to pay the extra taxes imposed to rebuild the destroyed dikes.[7] If Jordt experienced this disaster in coastal Burhave, then he would have had much to be bitter about. Memorials to the approximately eight hundred flood victims were later erected in many of the local churches.[8] A tradition of emigration is supposed to have started with the flood in certain districts of Holstein northeast of Burhave, and it was not limited to the coast only. Historian Paul-Heinz Pauseback wrote, "More and more people waited for an opportunity to leave the land."[9]

Jordt makes a point of calling himself a common man from the very beginning of his book, writing that he "belongs to that class of people in society for whom overpopulation made advancement in his fatherland too difficult." The theme of overpopulation is well known from this time; one contemporary was the dire English prognosticator Thomas Robert Malthus.[10] The population of Oldenburg city did not exhibit rapid growth until after the Napoleonic wars: its population in 1816 is given as 6,278, which increased to more than 9,400 in 1821, but the population was actually higher in 1769 than in 1816. It continued to grow and passed 15,000 in 1848.[11] Nevertheless, we do find traces of the problems caused by a slow-developing agricultural economy and the population increase outside of the city.

In the 1830s the government of the Grand Duchy of Oldenburg became concerned about the exodus to America. On July 11, 1834, the local authorities of Damme, south of the town of Oldenburg, were asked to report the number of persons who had emigrated since January 1, 1833, how much they had taken with them in valuables, and how many had returned or changed their minds before their ship left. The government also wanted to hear proposals for limiting emigration, and in the case of Damme to know why the number leaving the district was so high. The authorities of Damme emphasized three causes in their answer of July 31. The first was the disproportionate number of propertyless land tenants to landowners. All the land was owned by a few classes of people, and it was not being divided up. Since the class of land tenants was increasing rapidly, the contracts they had to endure were becoming more oppressive. Their situation was very insecure as they were competing for tenant contracts. The tenant could be hardworking and diligent, but he still was dependent on the landowner. Inappropriate services were demanded, and after working hard to improve bad land, he still risked being driven off and having to start all over in a new place. Under such circumstances, with no possibility of attaining their own land and no possessions to tie them down, many tenants decided to leave for other parts of the world where they might live a happier life.[12] Second, there were fewer sources of work for the lower classes than before. This was especially true in Holland, where many had once gone to find work, often on fishing boats or in the merchant fleet. Many people unable to find work in Holland returned even poorer than when they had left. Third, many in the area already had friends and family in America. They received invitations from overseas with exaggerated claims about the conditions. Those who said something negative about America were even accused of lying.

These were clear and insightful answers to the authorities' inquiries, and they are supported by modern research. Some years earlier, in 1817, 89.6 percent of those asked why they were emigrating from another German area answered that loss of property and valuables, lack of income opportunity, and hopes for a better life were motivating factors.[13] These concerns affected not only children of the poor but also those of the landowners, who had nothing to offer their younger children other than to become tenants at the family property while the oldest brother took over the undivided property ownership. Sons and daughters of the landowners were effectively declassed. America offered new opportunities, and those from landowning or business families had a better chance of raising the money for the journey than did the very poor. The situation was almost the opposite of what we are used to today; having money could not create a secure life locally, since the economy was heavily tilted toward land ownership. And money in most cases could not buy land; land was inherited by the oldest son. What money could do was to pay for a ticket out.

The situation was not better for those having a trade. With the generally depressed economy, there was little work to be had, and many tradesmen had to resort to tenant farming or try to get by in other ways.

The people living in Danish lands, as Jordt did until 1827, suffered extra taxes after the Danish state went bankrupt in 1813 under the pressure of the Napoleonic wars. The old currency was made worthless and an extra tax of 6 percent was levied on all property to pay for currency reform. There were no functioning banks left in Holstein. The result was a deep recession in which many farmers lost their land, eventually auctioning it off to pay taxes. The Danish government abandoned the unpopular currency reform in 1841 and went back to the old currency, but the price of the reform effort had been high, especially for the German part of the population. The Germans had paid higher taxes because the Danish state gave Danish speakers preferential treatment in an attempt to foster national identity.[14]

It should not be a surprise that Jordt did not do well in Holstein under the circumstances just described. He may have spent some of his time in the large Oldenburg library,[15] because he claims that he had

already read much about America, and for a long time the desire had been stirring in him [Jordt was writing about himself in the third person] to try his luck in that country as soon as possible, since almost all letters from earlier emigrants sounded favorable. However, he did not want simply to take his chances in so important an undertaking; on the contrary, his most fervent wish was that one of his closer acquaintances might settle there and that, for the time being, he could go there by himself and be instructed about everything he needed to know. Then, if the new country agreed with his desires, he would have his family follow. Fortune had not yet granted the author his wish, when the following letter [a letter from Friedrich Ernst at Mill Creek] arrived; and though he did not know the writer personally, he did hear enough from closer acquaintances and personal friends to recommend the man.[16]

One may wonder about these personal references of Ernst's, since he was accused of embezzling money from the post office by the Grand Duke of Oldenburg, but perhaps the locals knew something at that time that we do not know today. Ernst had worked for the duke as a gardener and a postal clerk. The duke died in 1829, the same year Ernst took his family and ran. The accusation may have had something to do with a new administrator taking over and conflicts arising from his reorganizations. We should take note that Ernst kept his status among people in Oldenburg. Visitors from German lands continued to write to Ernst for help and hospitality for as long as he lived.

When Jordt left Oldenburg he may have used parts of the new chaussee road between it and Bremen and taken a ferry from Brake to the new Bremen harbor close to the sea, called Bremerhaven. The opening of this harbor in 1830 and the new roads being built made it much faster and easier for emigrants from northern Germany to get to the coast and board the ships. Ship departures often took time. After Jordt boarded the *Leontine*, the ship stayed in harbor for four more weeks, leaving Bremerhaven on Christmas Eve of 1832. The voyage across the Atlantic took almost nine weeks.

After arriving in New York on February 22, 1833, Jordt traveled on to New Orleans, which he reached on March 20. He left that city on April 22, but it is not quite clear when he arrived in Texas. After a slow journey up the Brazos River, Jordt finally reached Bell's Landing. Counting the approximate days Jordt refers to in his narrative gives an arrival date of around May 20. But the actual date must have been ten to fifteen days earlier, given that he stayed at Martin Varner's settlement, where the Varner-Hogg State Historical Park is today, for three weeks and it was still May when he left. His arrival date cannot have been later than May 10, 1833. The riverboat could not get any farther upriver, so Jordt and another traveler acquired a small boat and set out for Varner's settlement. Jordt was a keen observer of nature, clearly in the romantic tradition of his age. He describes the beautiful evening and the not-so-beautiful mosquitoes at night, leading to a happy arrival at Varner's and the invitation to share breakfast. He stayed there while waiting for the roads to dry up and for a cold fever to let go. The cold fever, like the one that hit Burhave, may have been a malaria attack after experiencing the mosquitoes of the lower Brazos River. Jordt does not mention it, but we know that the roads were more than just wet. This was the time of the infamous 1833 flood and cholera epidemic. Jordt may have avoided the cholera by leaving the lower Brazos area in time and sitting it out in the remote Mill Creek settlement. He may not have wanted to tell his fellow Germans about the flood, since many in northern Germany were still reeling from their own flood of 1825. Like many Germans after him, Jordt did not fall in love with the lower Brazos region. He considered it unhealthy.

Starting out from Varner's to San Felipe, Jordt noticed the flatness of the prairie and the many ripe blackberries. He recorded that it was still May, much too early in the year for blackberries in Germany. Jordt's penchant for detail is a great advantage to us today since much that he could have taken for granted and simply skipped might otherwise be unknown to us. He informs us about the price he paid for one hundred pounds of freight from Varner's to San Felipe and tells us that his group of travelers set out with seven wagons, each drawn by six oxen. The wagons were slow, and Jordt took off along the road alone. This is perhaps something we don't think about today, that a human being would walk faster than a load of freight drawn by oxen, which was the normal arrangement. We might also consider the effect of the oxen on unimproved and wet trails over the prairie. There were good reasons to wait for the prairie to dry up.

On the first day from Varner's the party had their midday rest by a winding spring in what Jordt called a beautiful valley covered by shrubbery. This site could possibly be west of Damon, to the west of present-day State Highway 36. The travelers made coffee and pancakes, and Jordt expresses how much he enjoyed camping out during the trip. They stayed overnight at the Darst settlement. Jordt tells us that Darst (Abraham Dörst) knew Gottfried Duden in Missouri and that he ran a boardinghouse at the settlement. However, he advised his readers not to stay there or at any such house. The beds were not good, and since all travelers carried their own bedding anyway it was much better to sleep outdoors in the warm Texas climate. He also found a new friend at the Darst settlement, the Scottish botanist Thomas Drummond. Drummond had traveled in all parts of North America but had not found such an abundance of soil, vegetation, and easiness of livelihood anyplace other than in Texas. As we will see, Jordt would continue to describe nature and climate in highly positive phrases as long as he remained in Texas. He also found the traveling more and more pleasant as he got to know Mr. Drummond better. We may possibly assume that the botanist taught Jordt about plants and landscape, and that he found fertile ground for an educational tour de force in Jordt, who was keenly interested in his surroundings.

Jordt spent the last night before San Felipe in a Spanish settlement. He had lost his party and Mr. Drummond and ended up with people he had never seen before. He was a bit concerned at first, but he was treated well and put in a clean bed with mosquito netting. These were luxuries not mentioned at any other place. Jordt had heard that the Spanish were known for thievery and not for agriculture. Here he met honest, decent people who tended the land and kept a nice and welcoming home. This seems to have been confusing to him, since despite his experience he still claims later that the Spanish were good at horse thievery only.

Jordt describes San Felipe as something like a marketplace, with white buildings resembling tents and booths. As with so many other places in early Texas, today we have to imagine how it looked to a traveler on foot in 1833. Jordt describes the prairie at San Felipe as "very picturesque [. . .] here, alternating as it does with great variety between hills, valleys, and bushy areas." Modern observers might think the prairie appears flat when they arrive in San Felipe from the south. However, on foot one discovers that it is hillier than it seems, especially when approaching San Felipe from the southwest. Here there are rolling hills all the way into the old town.

Jordt describes the scenery in more detail in his story about looking for Bernard Scherrer's horse. Scherrer had been one of the travelers that came to Brazoria, but he left the party and went ahead to San Felipe. Jordt met him after wasting a day following the wrong trail out of town only to have to turn back after twelve miles. From his description, his turnaround point could have been at a crossing over the San Bernardo River. While looking for the horse they came upon Colonel Austin's house in a location Jordt called

the most beautiful one I had so far seen in Texas. Laid out in an attractive valley, before it there is a high gently rising elevation, covered in small sections with natural vegetation of oaks, mulberries, sycamores, etc., as if human hand had turned it into an English garden. In the background a creek clear as crystal runs in a deep bed through natural shrubbery and over rocks; at high water levels, it goes out of its banks and floods the immediate vicinity. However, one thing I regretted the house not having was a beautiful garden. It seems, generally speaking, that Americans only cherish whatever produces money and derive but little pleasure, even when wealthy, from such planned amenable installations, combining usefulness and beauty, and for which nature herself provides such vigorous encouragement.[17]

Austin was away on travel, Jordt reported. He does not mention that a political convention had been held right there in San Felipe the month before, from April 1 to April 13, 1833, or that Austin had left for San Antonio, Goliad, and ultimately Mexico City to deliver the resolutions of the convention. The changing relationship between Texas and the rest of Mexico was kept in the background by Jordt. He may not have wanted to bring attention to it, or he may have been unaware of the proceedings. Alternatively, it may have appeared that the situation was being resolved peacefully.

Jordt and his party left San Felipe around 4 p.m. and camped in a beautiful valley. The next day they traveled through wilder and even more beautiful terrain, with trees and plants that indicated productive soil. As they got closer to the Ernst settlement at Mill Creek, Jordt was reminded of the fields in eastern Holstein. There were "deceptive similarities in scenery."[18]

Jordt possibly arrived at Mill Creek by following the path of present-day Bermuda Road down to the settlement in Ernst Park. The valley is open there and a little creek ran through the old settlement. He described a hill with natural springs under some rocks to the south. The springs are still there, though perhaps they are no longer as attractive as in 1833. Pilgrim's Rest Cemetery is on the hill, with a larger cemetery area behind it. Ernst had diverted the springs down to the woods along Mill Creek to irrigate his garden and his cornfield. Jordt was in a state of total happiness, or at least he wanted his readers to see it that way:

> The high hill already mentioned provides a magnificent view of the natural romantic scenery, which nevertheless cannot be referred to as wilderness, there being nowhere a single plant of heather in sight. There is only green expanse, hills and valleys covered with individual stands of trees, high woodlands, brush, the most beautiful flowers, shining herds of cattle, and also flocks of deer. Against the horizon are hills and woodlands of still higher elevation, and an immense distance away there extends, through the deep valley of Mill Creek, a long band of primeval forest. Though the day after my arrival in this little Elysium had been intended for rest, in the company of Mr. Scherrer I climbed the hills nearest by, roamed about in

the woods, and there I had an invigorating bath in Mill Creek, which I enjoyed very much, having had for several years to forgo such pleasures because of lack of a suitable bathing site.[19]

This must have been like a description of paradise for tired, land-less, and frozen Oldenburgers reading Jordt's account a year later.

How well can we trust Jordt? Impressions are difficult to judge, and the physical landscape is as described. But there is a problem with the house. Jordt describes it as white and in the style of the Oldenburger garden house. Ernst himself also describes it as like a garden house. In interviews attached to the translation, Ernst's wife and daughter both say the house was very insubstantial, basi-cally a hut that could not be heated, nor was the roofing rainproof. There was no door and no windows for three years, and then a new and totally different house was built. The description of the house could fit a *jacal*-type hut built of upright sticks chinked with mud and clay and covered with a straw roof. Such a house could be built from sticks and straw collected locally and with mud from the creek. Jordt also makes a point of the nice climate; he slept out-doors under a tree, not in the house. On a visit to the neighbors the next day he comments that the Fordtran house was much more substantial than the Ernst house and sat high on top of a hill. The Ernst daughter remembered conditions as very basic for several years, and certainly no paradise.

But that is not what Jordt tells his readers:

I can assure all of my German countrymen with conviction that Mr. Ernst's letter, reproduced in the introduction, was completely confirmed in all particulars. Indeed, Texas is a country where conditions are made as easy for the immigrant who wants to pursue agriculture as they are anywhere else in the world, certainly to this extent—it is a land which puts riches in his lap, which can bring happiness to thousands and to their descendants—it is a country just waiting for people so that our European industry can raise and elevate it to the most blessed country in all the known world.[20]

Jordt was in the business of not only informing Germans about Texas but also marketing it to them. The Ernst family and their neighbors had much to gain from future immigration to the area. A league was far too much land for them to put to use. They would be better off selling parts of it. Their services would be in demand by immigrants, as travelers would need places to stay overnight, stores to supply them with goods, and mail service to keep them in touch with family overseas. The Ernst family ended up engaging in all of these activities, which formed the basis for the town of Industry. But could such developments be planned? Probably not to the degree suggested, but it does not seem unnatural to assume that Jordt and Ernst had long talks about the opportunities in Texas and the situation back in the fatherland. The unanswered question is what Jordt stood to gain. He had no land at this time, had not brought his family over, and was not eligible for the better land grant deals. The land office was closed anyway, and he wondered about the possibilities of a future grant area around the falls of the Brazos.[21] In the meantime, Jordt followed some of his own advice; he bought cattle and allowed it to roam on the land. He suggested to prospective immigrants that they would be welcome to make arrangements to cultivate some of the land of those who already had settled and to buy cattle while saving their money to look for their own piece of land.[22]

At this point in the book Jordt changes his focus from describing the journey and the landscape to advising new immigrants and explaining laws that promoted and regulated immigration in Texas. There were opportunities in Texas for thousands of Europeans, he wrote.

To this subject Jordt added a steady stream of reassurances to offset doubts prospective immigrants might have had about settling in a place that was still part of Mexico. There would be enough land for all. Schools—which Germans may have thought especially important given their long traditions of public schooling—could be established.[23] The German and Scandinavian tradition for well-organized schools was reflected in the literate Germans who immigrated to Texas. They knew how to read and write and calculate.

A number of them wrote books and articles similar to Jordt's about their travels to Texas and other states. Their audience in Europe was able to read and understand these works; empowered by their education, the readers were able to make decisions for themselves and their families based on words written far away.

As immigration increased, higher levels of cooperation developed among later Germans arriving in Texas. Germans began organizing themselves into immigration associations and communal groups to form settlements in their new homeland. Jordt mentions some cooperative efforts, but in his account they served only as a means to help travelers and newcomers, or perhaps as a way to build mutual aid among neighbors. There were still too few Germans in Texas at the time of Jordt's writing for any of the communal ideas and associations from home to spring to life.

Jordt devotes much of the latter part of his book to advising newcomers on how to clear and use the land. He often goes into considerable detail, making the book a practical guide for new settlers. He divides the soil into three types: cleared woodland, black prairie soil, and sandy prairie soil. The most productive and longest-lasting was the cleared woodland, but the work involved in removing the trees was so time-consuming, he writes, as to make this type of land less attractive than the black prairie soil. Jordt also informs his readers about the hard work involved in building fences. He estimates that a single acre required seven hundred to eight hundred logs four inches thick and ten feet long. An experienced worker could produce as many as 150 of these logs per day, but an immigrant would need time to learn the skills required.[24] Ernst had chosen a type of fence for his enclosure that required less wood:

> Along the line where the fence is to be erected, two posts of about two inches in diameter and five feet long are driven into the ground at four-and-a-half-foot intervals and half a foot apart; to make this easier, they are sharpened to a point at the lower end and sawed flush at the other. After one side of the field has been done, brush is placed between these posts along

the line and stamped solid; in this manner, a solid fence results, which is strengthened even further after a height of four
feet is attained, when for every nine feet—in other words,
at every other pair of posts—two posts are placed above in a
cross and hammered into the ground. Heavy posts are placed
in the crosses, and, in addition, above the fence, two ten-foot
posts crossing in such a manner that the upper end rests on
the crosses of the fence, with the lower ones crossing below
about two feet from the bottom of the fence. This way it is
impossible for the cattle to get close enough to the fence to
make a jump, even though they do not shun a five-foot height.
Nor can small domestic animals, such as young pigs, etc., get
through, as they do every day through the gaps of a rail fence
or enclosure."[25]

Jordt follows his account of building fences with a description of
how to plant a number of common crops.

What we have in Jordt's book is a little gemstone. It offers pure
entertainment and general knowledge about early Texas. It can be
read as a description of how early farms were established, or as a response to the social and economic realities in the German-speaking
lands of northern Europe at the time, thereby reflecting conditions
there as much as in Texas. It also can be read as an effort to market
Texas to the German-speaking population, perhaps in the hope of
gaining a profit from land and services, or perhaps simply to make
some money on the sale of the book.

Jordt returned to Oldenburg in the fall of 1834 and published
his book. According to Struve, he left for Texas again in February
1836, this time with his two sons, Hermann Emil Mathias, thirteen, and Karl Friedrich Sophus, fifteen. His wife, Dorothea, and
his two daughters, ages seven and ten, stayed behind. When Ernst
officiated the wedding of Jacob Wolters and Luisa Marie Wittwe
on April 6, 1841, Jordt and Peter Pieper, who owned a league of
land in Colorado County, were listed as witnesses. Six days later his
son Hermann Emil and several others were confirmed by Pastor

Louis Cachand Ervendberg during Easter services for the Industry, Cummins Creek, and Cat Springs district. Hermann Emil had followed the confirmation course from January 5 to April 10, 1841.[26] We also know that Friedrich Wrede was in Industry in early August 1841. He had bought some land at Cummins Creek unseen from a German in New Orleans and rode the nine miles from Industry to Cummins Creek, only to be deeply disappointed when he saw his purchase. Not knowing what to do, he went to Jordt and Pastor Ervendberg and asked them to help him.[27] Jordt's son Charles (Karl) Friedrich Sophus Jordt had been granted the right to 640 acres back in 1839,[28] but his property had not been surveyed. Wrede paid him an extra twenty dollars and swapped his land for Jordt's land in a deal they went to Columbus to register on August 9, 1841.[29] The land was in the eastern part of the Matthews League, about one mile east of Cummins Creek. Charles Jordt later bought more land in Colorado County from Wrede and others. He bought property from his father-in-law Samuel Redgate in 1851,[30] from Wilhelm Frels in 1853,[31] and from his brother Hermann in May 1859.[32]

Detlef Thomas Friedrich Jordt also acquired land in 1841, buying sixty acres from Jacob Wolters in Piepers League that year.[33] On Good Friday three years later, in 1844, his sons Hermann Emil and Charles were both communicants. Later the same year Charles Jordt and Johann Ernst, the son of Friedrich Ernst of Industry, were both hired by Prince Solms-Braunfels as guides and hunters.[34] At this time the father is not mentioned, but he may have been back in Oldenburg since he was present at his daughter's confirmation in Bockhorn that year. His occupation was listed as innkeeper in Berne/Wesermarsch, which may have been the occupation of his wife, since Detlef spent so much time traveling. The last known record of Detlef Jordt was in September 1847, when Friedrich Ernst officiated at the wedding of his daughter Henriette. She and her mother had come to Texas the year before with the daughter's groom-to-be. Jordt senior died in the same year and is believed to be buried in Columbus.

The Jordt family continued to live in Colorado County. Hermann Emil was among the original twenty-five trustees of Calvary College. He was elected president of the Hermann University (Seminary) in Frelsburg in 1860 and owned the two lots north of Trinity Lutheran Church at that time.[35] He was justice of the peace in Frelsburg.[36] During the Civil War, volunteers from Colorado County formed a company on April 7, 1862, and elected Hermann Jordt captain.[37] The company became Company H in the Seventeenth Texas Volunteer Infantry Regiment. It fought at Milliken's Bend, Louisiana, on June 7, 1863. Jordt died on July 22, 1863. Neither the location nor the cause of his death is known. His wife, Jane, was granted sole and exclusive rights when his will was finally probated after the war.[38]

Charles Jordt ran a store in Frelsburg in 1850,[39] even though he was a citizen of Columbus.[40] He still ran the store in 1860. Thirty years after Detlef Jordt came to Texas to inspect the land Friedrich Ernst wrote about, his family was well integrated in Colorado County. They owned land and a store, they had fought for Texas, and grandchildren had been born. Henriette Jordt and her husband, Theodor Hardi, welcomed their son Louis Carl Heinrich on January 31, 1861. Charles (Karl) Jordt and Antoinette Malstädt had a daughter named after her mother on July 25, 1861. Hermann Emil and Jane Redgate had Carl Louis Emmil on May 24, 1862. "Detlef Dunt" and his descendants had come to stay.

A NOTE ON THE TRANSLATION

The reader will find in the text a number of square brackets with information or corrections. This is the work of Mr. Saustrup and was done during the original translation. They have been kept in place since they often provide the modern reader with much-needed information and clarification. The translator retained Dunt's spelling of names but put the correct spelling in brackets.

Figure 2. The Kollmann store in Frelsburg originally belonged to the Jordt family. Kollmann bought the store before the Civil War. Courtesy of the Nesbitt Memorial Library Archives.

Figure 3. Detlef Thomas Jordt was an investor and sponsor of Hermann University, which became Hermann Seminary in Frelsburg. So were both his sons, Karl Friedrich Sophus (1820–1879) and Hermann Emil Mathias (1822–1863; Civil War casualty). Picture from 1890. Courtesy of the Nesbitt Memorial Library Archives.

Figure 4. Old Columbus Cemetery is the final resting place of Dorothea
(Heeder) Jordt (1802–1870), widow of Detlef Thomas Friedrich Jordt,
and their oldest son, Karl Friedrich Sophus Jordt (1820–1879). It is
believed that Detlef Thomas Friedrich Jordt is buried there also.
Photo by James C. Kearney.

NOTES

1. Anders Saustrup, introduction to a translation of *Voyage to Texas*, unpublished manuscript, 11–12.

2. Walter Struve, "Detlef Dunt," in *Germany and the Americas: Culture, Politics and History*, ed. Thomas Adam (Santa Barbara, CA: ABC-CLIO, 2005), 285–287. Unless otherwise noted, the following biographical data are extracted from the article by Struve.

3. "Othere's Voyage to the White Sea," http://viking.no/e/travels/navigation /e-ottar.htm. Accessed September 27, 2013.

4. http://www.gilde-luetjenburg.de/html/fruhgeschichte.html. Accessed September 27, 2013.

5. Dorothea Jordt, née Heeder, ca. 1802–January 11, 1870, is buried in Columbus City Cemetery.

6. Detlef Dunt, *Reise nach Texas*, p. 39 in this book.

7. Heie Focken Eichinger, "Deichbau und Küstenschutz in früheren Jahrhunderten," in *Ostfriesland und das Land Oldenburg im Schutz der Deiche*, ed. Christoph Ohlig, 31–44, Schriften der Deutschen Wasserhistorischen Gesellschaft, Band 6 (2004)(?). See http://books.google.com/books?id=VZoz nZGDm6IC&printsec=frontcover#v=onepage&q=&f=false. Accessed September 27, 2013.

   For a contemporary analysis, see A. D. Cramer, *Grundriß der Stadt Emden mit Bezeichnung der Verwüstungen der Sturmfluth des 3ten und 4ten Febr. 1825, nebst Beilage* (Oldenburg 1827).

8. Hans Poppe, *Zwischen Elms und Weser, Land und Leute in Oldenburg und Ostfriesland* (Oldenburg und Leipzig, 1888), 263. See also http://runne.net/ru dolf.folkerts/sturmfluten.html. Accessed September 27, 2013.

9. Paul-Heinz Pauseback, "Immer mehr Menschen wartelen bald nur noch auf eine Gelegenheit, um das Land zu verlassen." http://www.geschichte-s -h.de/vonabisz/auswanderung.htm. Accessed September 27, 2013.

10. Thomas Robert Malthus (1766–1834) was an English scholar and demographer who predicted a catastrophe if the population increase continued.

11. Stadt Oldenburg, Statistik Bevölkerung, Tabell 0201. Entwicklung der Einwohnerzahl 1702–2012. www.oldenburg.de/fileadmin/oldenburg/Ben utzer/PDF/40/402/0201-2-2012-Internetx.pdf.

12. Johannes Ostendorf, *Zur Geschichte der Auswanderung aus dem alten Amt Damme (Oldbg.)*. See http://www.honkomp.de/damme-auswanderung/kap itel3.htm. Accessed September 27, 2013.

13. Wolfgang Von Hippel, Tabelle 33, repr. in Christina Schleifenbaum, *Struktur der Auswanderung*, Seminararbeit 2000; see http://www.grin.com/e-book /98312/struktur-der-auswanderung. Accessed September 27, 2013.

14. http://www.geschichte-s-h.de/vonabisz/staatsbankrott.htm. Accessed September 27, 2013.

15. The Oldenburg library had sixty thousand books ten years later, in 1844. It was and is a public library dedicated to the education of the people.
16. Dunt, *Reise nach Texas*, p. 29 in this book.
17. Ibid., 82.
18. Ibid., 84.
19. Ibid., 84–85.
20. Ibid., 85.
21. Ibid., 88, 99–100.
22. Ibid., 86–87.
23. In Jordt's time schooling was both a right and an obligation for children in his homeland. The Danish king had introduced a school law in 1646, and by 1805 an organized system of public schools had become a reality.
24. Dunt, *Reise nach Texas*, 111 in this book.
25. Ibid., 111–112.
26. *Nesbitt Memorial Library Journal (NMLJ)* 2, no. 1 (January 1992): 57.
27. Friederich von Wrede Sr., *Lebensbilder aus den Vereinigten Staaten von Nordamerika und Texas* (Kassel: Emil Dresher, 1844), 184.
28. *NMLJ* 3, no. 3 (September 1993): 145; Charles F. S. was granted second-class conditional certificate number 32 on September 5, 1839, for 640 acres upon demonstrating by declaration of Colin DeBland and Detlef Thomas Friedrich Jordt (his father—the author) that he had resided in Texas in September 1836, i.e., for three years.
29. Colorado County, Reverse Deed Record, Book G, 155–156, August 9, 1841. Three tracts, 200 acres each. Deed recorded September 18, 1849.
30. Colorado County, Reverse Deed Record, Book G, 480, May 8, 1851.
31. Colorado County, Reverse Deed Record, Book H, 567, August 10, 1853.
32. Colorado County, Reverse Deed Record, Book K, 158, May 2, 1859.
33. Colorado County, Reverse Deed Record, Book C, 132–133, June [no date], 1841. See also *NMLJ* 6, 80. The property was at the south line of the league, from the south side of the creek going south 2,170 varas, or 6,028 feet.
34. James C. Kearney, *Nassau Plantation: The Evolution of a Texas German Slave Plantation* (Denton: University of North Texas Press, 2010), 82.
35. *NMLJ* 7, 25n38. Also see p. 27 and map showing Frelsburg lot owners as of October 1860.
36. Ibid., 40.
37. Ibid., 88 and 125 (muster roll).
38. Colorado County, Probate Index, no. 487, 44, H. E. Jordt, December 26, 1865, rights granted, and April 30, 1866, probate date.
39. *NMLJ* 7, 40 and 58 (census 1860).
40. *NMLJ* 4, 56.

Reise nach Texas,

nebst

Nachrichten von diesem Lande;

für Deutsche,

welche nach Amerika zu gehen beabsichtigen.

———

Herausgegeben

von

Detlef Dunt.

Bremen, 1834.

Gedruckt bei Carl Wilh. Wiehe.

Figure 5. The title page of *Reise nach Texas.*

Journey to Texas, Including Information about This Country, for Germans Intending to Go to America.

Detlef Dunt

Translated by Anders Saustrup

PREFACE

MUCH HAS BEEN WRITTEN about America, but as far as I know nothing as yet about Texas;[1] it would have been desirable if more had been known about this country at an earlier time, since many individuals would then be better off than is now the case—people who left their dear German fatherland convinced that they would improve their circumstances in America, but who in the northern areas, in the United States, instead found their advancement made even more difficult than at home. It is indeed to be lamented how, in many instances, working-class Germans with such little fore-thought take the important step of tearing themselves away from everything which has bound them to their fatherland. The some-times quite exaggerated descriptions by countrymen, who often write so favorably only for their own interest, prompt those poor people to perceive nothing but an Eldorado in the New World, and subsequently they must often find themselves painfully disap-pointed. Nevertheless, I have become acquainted with several in-dividuals who, at the time they set foot on American soil, still did not know which one of the states on this enormous continent they wanted to go to, and were still completely unfamiliar with the circumstances here. Such poor people really deserve pity, and there is an urgent need to inform them better about what advantages they can expect in the New World. The purpose of these pages is to warn my German brothers in the fatherland against ill-advised emigration plans and—once they have considered everything and firmly resolved to seek their happiness in the New World—to show them the course I think they should follow in order not to regret this important step, separated as they will be from their fatherland by the enormous Atlantic Ocean. My pen will be guided by the strongest desire for truth, and it is my most fervent wish to be of use to my fine German countrymen by way of these pages. I shall consider myself very fortunate if through this little book I could provide better opportunity and a better situation for the many worthy heads of families denied the means of subsistence by their fatherland. However, I hope to God and am firmly convinced that particularly in this state [Coahuila and] Texas, thousands more— provided they do not come here with exaggerated expectations— will, in return for moderate physical work, find a carefree existence and an honest living.

Written at the Friedrich Ernst settlement on Mill Creek,
in Austin's Colony, in the state of [Coahuila and] Texas in
New Mexico [Mexico], in September, 1833.

THE CAUSES OF the now so widespread emigration are highly varied; one person finds them in political offenses, whereas another, particularly if belonging to the younger segment of the population, is egged on by the urge to see the world. However, in the majority of cases it is assuredly the overpopulation of our beloved fatherland. It is so tempting to find the cause in the taxation practices, which are admittedly rather severe in some German states, and consequently throw the blame on the ruling princes. It should be kept in mind, however, that many honorable men may certainly still be found among these, who would like to ease their subjects of such burdens, if only their situation with respect to other states, the location of the country, etc., permitted this. Many people here, in a free America, would gladly pay more taxes if they had the fine roads, good police protection, etc., enjoyed in Germany under many truly good and honorable ruling princes. A lot more could probably be said about this particular point had it been in keeping with the intention of these pages. Those resolved to seek their happiness in the New World should above all else carefully examine whether they can prevail in their fatherland at all—for certainly they will overestimate many things in America that can be realized only with difficulty. Many who could live quiet, satisfied lives in their familiar settings regret too late that they have given up a secure subsistence for an uncertain one. Secondly, every emigrant would do well to test his physical capabilities, to make sure he can endure what hardships, deprivations, and physical labor might be required. Thirdly, concern about a good supply of ready money is not to be disregarded; regrettably, many fail to consider this sufficiently. As a conclusion to this brief introduction, I must—fourthly—make a note that it is altogether necessary to make a firm travel plan and stick to it. Here, as well as in the United States, I came to know many Germans who, trusting to their good luck, went to New York, Baltimore, Charlestown [Charleston], etc., then traveled in this state or that in order to explore everything, partly on the basis of vague information. The result was that they often found themselves disappointed and—saddest of all—spent their fine money on travel and subsequently must now make their living on a daily wage.

DEPARTURE FROM OLDENBURG FOR NEW YORK BY WAY OF BREMERHAVEN, WITH PERTINENT OBSERVATIONS.

Report of a Letter from an Oldenburg Man in Texas. Description of New York, etc.

THE PRESENT AUTHOR also belongs to that class of people in society for whom overpopulation made advancement in his fatherland too difficult. He had already read much about America, and for a long time the desire had been stirring in him to try his luck in that country as soon as possible, since almost all letters from earlier emigrants sounded favorable. However, he did not want simply to take his chances in so important an undertaking; on the contrary, his most fervent wish was that one of his closer acquaintances might have settled there and that, for the time being, he could join there by himself and be instructed about everything he needed to know. Then, if the new country agreed with his desires, he would have his family follow. Fortune had not yet granted the author his wish when the following letter arrived; and though he did not know the writer personally, he did hear much from closer acquaintances and personal friends to recommend the man. The letter in question is too important not to be presented to the reader, so it will be given the small space needed here and rendered in its entirety:

From a Settlement on Mill Creek in Austin's Colony in the
state of [Coahuila and] Texas in New Mexico [Mexico]

In keeping with my request, the travel account that I sent to
my brother-in-law right after our arrival in New York will
have been shared with all of you. It contained everything that
I considered necessary to report. At that time I had nothing to
say about America, but now that I have spent more than two
years on this continent and so far have traveled more than
1,400 miles across it, I can at least tell you what should be especially useful to emigrants; these few sheets of writing paper
do not allow room for more, and even so I shall have to be
brief, so without further ado, I'll set out right away. It will be
mentioned only in passing that we went by way of Münster,
Wesel, Maastricht, Brussels, Ostend, Dunkirk, Abbeville, and
Dieppe to Havre-de-Grâce, and from there crossed the Atlantic Ocean on a packet ship to New York within four weeks,
and reached this immeasurable city with its two hundred
thousand inhabitants. However, in the north the United States
does not offer immigrants its former advantages. Here we
found winter to be just as severe as in Germany, for which reason we decided to go farther south. Accordingly, we took ship
in February and went to New Orleans on a brig. Even though
it was severe winter right at our departure from New York,
nevertheless on the fourth day after our leave the mild air of
spring was already wafting toward us, and three days later, between Cuba and Florida, we had veritable summer, which per-
sisted the entire distance of one thousand nautical miles across
that part of the ocean, through the Bahama Bay [Florida
Straits] into the Gulf of Mexico, right to the mouth of the
Missisippi [Mississippi]. Our brig was towed 120 miles up to
New Orleans by a steamship, which already had two brigs and
one schooner in tow. In New Orleans we received favorable
reports about Texas and Austin's Colony located there, so we
took passage on a thirty-seven-ton schooner, the *Satillo*, which

already had more than one hundred people on board, and after a week-long trip landed at Harrisburg in this colony. Every immigrant who wants to farm receives a league of land if he arrives with wife or family, or if as a single man, a quarter-league; sons over fourteen years of age have identical claims on land distribution. A league is an hour's journey long and just as wide; in return he must defray 160 dollars in regular payments for surveyor's fees, installation costs, etc., must take the oath of citizenship, and after the course of a year is a free citizen of the free United States of Mexico. As Europeans who are especially welcome, we, too, received a league of land in this same manner and settled there; that is where I'm writing this letter from. The state [province] of Texas, of which our colony constitutes almost one-sixth, is located to the south, on the Gulf of Mexico, between the 27th° and the 31st° northern latitude; previously followers of Napoleon had settled here at Camp d'Asile. Austin's Colony is traversed by the Trinidad, Río Brazos, and Río Collorado [Colorado] rivers; within it are situated the major seat of St. Felippe [San Felipe] de Austin and the townships of Harrisburg, Brazoria, and Matagorda. Tampico and Vera Cruz can be reached by sail in three to four days. The land is undulating and alternates between woodlands and expanses of native grass. They are showy with the most wonderful flowers and blossoms, such as magnolias. The meadows have the most sumptuous stands of grass; I should have been able to sell several thousand cartloads of hay, if there had only been takers; but instead of being mowed it is burned off in late summer. The soil is so rich it never requires fertilizing. The climate resembles that of lower Italy; during the summer it is admittedly warmer than in Germany, because we have the sun almost directly overhead. On the other hand, it is not nearly as hot as might be presumed, since a persistent fresh east breeze cools the air; moreover, in the summertime there is not much to do, and people wear light clothing such as white cotton trousers and vests. In winter, like right now, the weather is usually what Germany has during the first two weeks of spring in March. Only twice so far, when the wind was blowing hard from the northwest, have we had freezing ice. In an entire month the weather will prevent fieldwork only for a couple of days. The sun and air are always bright and clear; bees and butterflies are seen year round, birds are singing in the shrubs, some of which are evergreen; and in winter as well as in summer the cattle find their own feed. The cows calve without assistance and come home at night to suckle their calves, which are kept in the daytime in an area protected by a wooden fence. In this way the return of the cows is assured. Calves are never slaughtered. A cow with calf costs ten dollars. There are one hundred cents to a dollar, so a cent is about equal to an Oldenburg Grote. Horses cost somewhat more and are only used for riding; everybody rides, whether male or female. Oxen are used for draft animals and plowing. There are farmers here who own close to seven hundred head of cattle. But the rate of propagation is also quite extraordinary, and young cows of 1¾ years of age already bring calves into the world. Hogs increase so astonishingly that, beginning with six, you may have one hundred the following year; they, too, cost nothing to maintain, since they find abundant feed in the woods and only occasionally are given a few kernels of corn to get them used to the house. Moreover, pork is at a good price with four dollars per hundred pounds. A local immigrant bought six sows two years ago; after breeding them he has now sold eighty fat hogs, each one of them over two hundred pounds. Generally speaking, all agricultural products fetch a good price greatly to the farmer's advantage. Corn, or Turkish wheat, costs seventy-five cents to a dollar per bushel[2] and is as good as cash money—of which there is not much in circulation, since everything is transacted by barter. On one *Morgen* [acre] of good land, which can be plowed in one day, thirty to forty bushels of corn will grow, for which the seed corn can be planted by children. Fields for planting are protected by split wooden enclosures so the cattle won't ruin anything, since they are allowed to run at large. The products cultivated here consist of sugarcane, cotton of best quality, tobacco, rice, indigo—which grows wild around here—corn, *batatas* or sweet potatoes, melons of exceptional quality, watermelons, pumpkins, wheat, rye, all kinds of garden vegetables, and peaches in great quantity. Moreover, growing wild in the woods are mulberries, several kinds of walnut, persimmons as sweet as honey, and grapes in large quantity but not of outstanding taste. Honey is frequently found in hollow tree trunks, where bee swarms settle; there are birds of all kinds, from pelicans to hummingbirds, and game such as deer, bears, raccoons, opossum, wild turkeys, geese, ducks, and partridges—these last-mentioned are in quantity and as large as domestic chickens; they are actually gray pheasants. From our house in particular, we daily see flocks of game grazing. Moreover, there is free hunting everywhere, and very delicate fish, sometimes weighing forty pounds. There are also herds of foxes as well as of wild horses, which can be captured as colts and tamed. There are also wolves here, but of such a timid sort that they flee from my youngest children. Although a panther or leopard may be seen from time to time, predators are, generally speaking, not dangerous. I have wandered for days alone in the deepest thicket, where no human had set foot before, without ever seeing any such animal; on the other hand, the hunting bounty is always great and provides us with the most exquisite roasts. The meadows are adorned with the most beautiful, gorgeous flowers, some of which I never saw before, and which in Germany can only be grown in a greenhouse; I feel ashamed to scatter the seeds brought from home where the carpet of meadowland displays a continuous show of flowers. There are also many kinds of snakes here, among them the rattlesnake, several of which I have killed. How little they are noticed is proved by the fact that many a hunter or herdsman walks barefoot all summer long, through all kinds of tall grass and brush, without even thinking of snakes. Furthermore, everybody knows remedies for the bites of such animals; three times I have seen people bitten, but never anyone die from it. In view of the large landholdings, it is obvious that the inhabitants cannot be living closely together; nevertheless my closest neighbor lives only ten minutes from my house, since we both have settled not far from our property line. A league of land comprises 4,444 [4,428] acres[3] or *Morgen*, consisting of hilly areas and valleys, woods and meadows cut through by small creeks, and when there are several settlements in one location the value of land is such that acreage has already been sold at one dollar. As in the United States the constitution of this country is free, and political quarrels are unknown to us here; still, by way of a newspaper regularly published at San Antonio on the Rio del Norte, we are informed of every world event. The English language is quickly learned; my wife and I, and my children in particular, can already manage fairly well, and I read the newspaper as well as I do a German one. Although the introduction of slaves is prohibited, keeping them is tacitly tolerated since there would otherwise be a shortage of laborers, because of it being so easy to earn a living. Workingmen earn seventy-five cents to a dollar a day with board. All items of clothing and footwear are expensive, so almost everyone makes his own. In general, everybody lives in the open and by himself, so there is little need for cash money; thus I am quite happy finally to have my wishes fulfilled and find myself in a position where I can do everything according to my preferences. Everybody builds his own house, either by himself or with help from his neighbors; not much is spent on its beauty, rather it is only constructed of hewn wooden logs. Mine was built—with the assistance of my son Fritz, who can already cut down tree trunks two feet thick—on the order of my former garden house in Oldenburg, but on a larger scale. Working regularly in the open has made me healthier and stronger than I ever was in Germany, and my wife is blooming like a rose, as are the children. My son Hermann is growing exceptionally and turning into a genuine Mexican. They all have their rustic chores: Lina already milks her three cows, Fritz and Louis help me with farming, and the younger ones have various jobs such as planting and picking cotton, which is exceedingly easy since it grows like weeds. Every day fresh cornbread is made in an iron pot with a fireproof lid, and it tastes like the finest rice cakes. Our corn is of far better quality than in Germany; I grind it in a very simple manner and it yields not only meal but also shelled groats, like rice. Meat, which, from every kind of animal, is much tastier than in Germany, is eaten fried in the morning at breakfast, as well as at noon and in the evening. There are mosquitoes here just as in all warmer regions. Those who have been bitten by gnats on the German moors will consider this American nuisance worse over there than here. They are more frequent on the coast, but since we are living more than one hundred miles inland, where it is hillier and airier, we have little of this. In general I have no feeling of disadvantage except the great distance from my friends; if I could conjure them up, I would have heaven on earth. From the faithful description above, you will realize what advantages the farmer here has over the farmer over there; a free constitution and, for the time being, no local taxes whatever and later only slight ones; easy cattle raising, hardly three months of real work, no fertilizing of the acreage, no gathering of winter feed, no need for money, easy construction of houses and making of clothes, etc.; free hunting and game aplenty; everywhere free exercise of religion, etc.; all of this—with the best market for his products—combines to make the farmer happy and, in a few years, affluent. This is proved by everybody who has been here for four to six years. Up higher on the rivers there are beautiful areas, and silver has been found there; it is merely a matter of driving off an Indian tribe that resists individual visits. Several Indian tribes are moving about peacefully like Cossacks, hunting deer, of which they sell the hides. If some of you, my friends, or anybody else should decide, after reading this letter, to enjoy undisturbed freedom here and head for an assured pleasant future—instead of waiting until those few tangible possessions that remain vanish completely and thus being deprived of the means for passage—then let me offer the following advice with regard to the journey: book passage in steerage on one of the ships plying from the Weser River to New Orleans. I do not know the fare exactly, but it should not exceed forty-five dollars per person, since it would then be preferable to go to New York (costs thirty-five dollars and from there to New Orleans ten dollars, personal belongings free). From New Orleans to Texas (Harrisburg) ten dollars. Belongings are paid separately. Families should try for a discount; children usually pay half fare. You buy your own provisions. If the wind is favorable, the trip to New Orleans can be made in five to six weeks, and from there to Harrisburg in four days. Take passage so that you don't arrive in New Orleans between July and October, since yellow fever is prevalent there at that time. Once in Harrisburg, hire a wagon for San Felipe and report at the land office. It is safest to travel with several others, with one of them knowing the English language or studying it up to the time of departure. Each one must help the others, and if any of you only brings enough money to manage the very essential initial purchases, then what another among you may be paying beyond his share can soon be equalized. The head of a family must keep well in mind that the league of land granted him amounts to receiving as much land as a noble count owns, with an immediate value of six hundred to eight hundred dollars, at which price leagues have often been sold here already. Incidentally, the expenses for the land do not have to be paid immediately, and may be paid in cattle, which they raise themselves here. For my friends and other known countrymen I have, for the moment, enough room on my property, until they have the leisure to look for an unoccupied league, which does take time; however, Colonel Austin recently promised that such Germans as might arrive are to be well situated. An unmarried man should bring a woman who is not swayed by external appearances and what is fashionable. You, my dear C., have already experienced many setbacks in the world, which may cause you to wish for all memories to be erased. So, if there is any way to make this possible, do not delay for a moment coming over here with your loved ones; your brother, Hermann, who understands agriculture so thoroughly, would quickly be in his true element here. However, for professional people there is no particular prospect here. Bring your sisters; young girls can very well find their happiness here. If everybody comes whom I used to call a friend, nobody will lose anything by the exchange; next summer I will be building a house for prospective arrivals and will grow some fruit. May I soon have the pleasure of both being used quite shortly by friends; how happy that would make me. I expect no reply to this letter; communication from here is too difficult and uncertain. Come yourself and bring me letters from those who stayed behind; that would be the greatest joy for me. Once arrived in San Felipe, any of you should inquire about Friedrich Ernst on Mill Creek. Passports are nowhere required. My wife begs of your wife not to be afraid of the ocean voyage; at first she was so fearful she wouldn't go on board, but now that she has made two ocean voyages with me, she would surely travel with me around the world. Apart from a few gales, we didn't have a single misfortune and were barely seasick. Next August, when somebody from over there may possibly show up, our hopes will be stirring, and we shall believe it will be dear friends whenever a wagon arrives. Although the ocean and unanticipated bitter events separate us, I have still never ceased to be moved when I think of you, my dear friends, and you live daily in my heart.

Your

Fritz

The letter above could not fail to cause a great sensation in the Old-enburg lands, which on the whole are but a poor country, all the more so since within the past year the desire to emigrate had been spreading even this far. Many copies were made of the letter. At least as far as Oldenburg is concerned, it would thus not have been necessary for me to reproduce it here, had I not been prompted on the one hand by the many spurious copies in circulation and on the other by the desire to make it known in other regions. After I was finally fortunate enough to have this letter in hand, which, considering how scant copies were at the time, was not so easy, my decision was made immediately, and I did not delay it for a mo-ment. However, a pleasant yet sad duty still confronted me: taking leave of relatives and friends living distant in the country. Those will always remain unforgettable days for me, spent in the circle of these loved ones; and though my desire was great to start my journey soon, still I have to thank my fortune that I did not find a ship right away. Finally—it was on November 20 of last year—the hour struck when duty demanded that I separate for the time being from my wife and children. Indeed I had often been appre-hensive of this sad hour, but I had never imagined the pain would be so sharp. My eyes become wet again whenever I think of that scene, with the children hanging around my neck and my wife hav-ing to remind me to get hold of myself. But enough of this; those who are husbands and fathers will be capable of imagining my pain in that bitter hour of parting. Saying good-bye to my old father-in-law, an aged, dignified veteran of seventy-two years, shook me deeply since I had always loved him as would a child. Now the hardest part had been overcome, and I was determined henceforth to bear whatever Providence might still have in store for me. To-gether with a friend, a Mr. S., I went to Bremen the same evening; he too had decided, for the time being, to go alone with me to Mr. Ernst's in Texas. At the house of Wätjen & Co. in Bremen, owners and chief freighters of the ship *Leontine*, which was bound for New York and commanded by Captain Grau [Diedrich Graue], we paid for our passage and received instructions to be on board the ship at

Bremerhaven not later than November 28. It was a stormy morning with continuous snow when I arrived in Brake. After I had been waiting for about half an hour in the appointed inn, Mr. Schwarting also arrived; he had still had some relatives to say goodbye to. Around one o'clock in the afternoon the weather cleared and we went straightaway with our things down to Bremerhaven on a sailing barge from Blankenese, arriving around seven o'clock at night in complete darkness. We reported immediately to Captain Graue, where we got the not very comforting news that we would probably by lying there for another four weeks. Nevertheless, with our passage confirmed and consequently the obligation of the ship to us begun, we boarded the very next day. Indeed, the captain had spoken the truth; we remained lying there almost until Christmas Eve. Although I was bored, I endeavored to spend my time as well as possible with reading, correspondence to my friends, and walking tours to Bremerlehe and Gestendorf [Geestendorf]. Finally, on a foggy, dark December morning—it happened to be on a Sunday—we went to the roadstead, where we remained the rest of the day. The following morning, by the gray of dawn, we were already under sail. Only then did it occur to me that it was Christmas Eve; I felt very stirred by this coincidence, and it seemed to me that a journey undertaken on the day when the Savior of the world was born could only mean good luck. The ship went through the waves rather fast, and since I was feeling quite comfortable, I used this time to write my wife once again and was able to send my letter with the pilot from Bremen who was on board. For quite some time we could still see the Oldenburg coastline and the churches of Burhave and Langwarden. I cannot express what feelings overcame me upon seeing this. I had previously lived for two years in the first-mentioned church village, and so many memories of pleasures enjoyed there, as well as bitter pain, unintentionally became associated with the view of that coast and that church tower.

My company in steerage consisted of just five persons, indeed a great relief during the long ocean voyage, since it is surely extremely calamitous and uncomfortable to be squeezed together with too

many passengers. The good pilot, a certain Nothholz [Harm Diedrich Nothholt] whom I had known when he was attached to the
Oldenburg pilot service, left us after we had passed somewhat beyond the so-called Bremen beacon. After we had all given him the
correspondence items for our loved ones, we took quite a heart-
felt leave of him. My companion, Mr. Schwarting, had already felt
some discomfort from the voyage during the day, with quite severe
vomiting, so he was confined to his bed all day long. It was about
eight o'clock in the evening, while I was sitting quite comfortably
in steerage and still making jokes of how I would apparently remain quite free of that discomfort, when I, too, strangely enough—
almost as a punishment for my overconfidence—suddenly had to
surrender. However, after this emptying-out I felt quite relieved
and lay down in bed right away on the advice of a cabin passenger. During the night the wind turned considerably stronger, but
I still slept quite well. Upon waking up in the morning, we had a
regular gale; I thought to myself, when once again I felt somewhat
uncomfortable, that Christmas Day would probably not bring me
any particular joy, and that is indeed what happened. The first joy
was a second attack of vomiting, but not at all severe. Though I
now felt quite relieved, I was still quite weak and had appetite for
neither eating nor drinking. In the afternoon I finally got out of my
berth and tumbled toward the staircase to the cabin to watch the
wild dance of the waves. The terrifyingly beautiful view certainly
made quite a striking impression, particularly for somebody who
had never seen such a spectacle; however, I shall shun any description of these stark nature scenes, as to form an adequate impression
it is necessary to see for oneself. Moreover, hundreds before me
have expressed themselves, in prose or poetry, about this subject.
Apart from some weakness in my limbs, I had by now overcome
the seasickness and developed some appetite again. On this occasion I cannot but recommend the following simple procedure for
seasickness to anybody who is on an ocean voyage for the first time.
Once you have vomited and feel comfortable and relieved, go to
bed right away; but don't do this if you don't feel quite comfortable

Figure 6. Jordt's ship, the *Leontine*, departed from the new harbor of Bremerhaven on Christmas Eve 1832. By then Jordt had already spent four weeks waiting on board. By permission of the Historisches Museum Bremerhaven.

at the moment. Many adopt the habit of going to bed upon the slightest feeling of discomfort; this is an entirely wrong approach. You should stay about until you reach the point of vomiting; then you will feel at ease and should not delay finding your comfortable bed. Generally, you should guard against going to bed too frequently and hold out instead as long as possible and, weather permitting, go on deck; if you don't follow this rule, you will never get your sea legs. All of us, following the captain's instructions, quickly got accustomed to the sea, even the wife of one of our travel companions. Only one individual did not want to heed and thus had the distinction of getting seasick whenever the ship made a sharp movement. Subsequently, I never enjoyed better sleep than when a gale broke out in the middle of the night, but then I did not delay either in getting out of my bed as soon as possible.

For some days now nothing whatever of note happened; the ship moved quickly through the waves, and little by little I accustomed myself to life at sea. The following Sunday afternoon we could see the coastline of France, and in the darkness of the New Year's Eve the beautiful gas lighting of Dover was shining toward us. In steerage we celebrated this evening with a frugal dish of pancakes. How vividly I was thinking of that evening which I had often spent so joyously in the circle of my loved ones, and I wished for blessings and health and happiness to descend on them. The English Channel was now passed in a few days without anything of importance happening, and we then safely reached the immense Atlantic Ocean. A long sea voyage has, in effect, many everyday aspects about it, and not much of interest can be reported, at least not anything that has not already been said by earlier travelers; I hope, therefore, to be of more use to my good readers by acquainting them with the actual way of life on ships and with the essentials to be brought from Europe to better one's comfort during the voyage.

Baron von Knigge has written a book about social conduct. As is well known, in this book he has expressed himself about behavior in all situations of human life, particularly about travel deportment. However, he may well have forgotten one case in point, and that is conduct on ocean voyages. In this instance he is undoubtedly to be excused, however, since he may never have made a voyage of any consequence.

You enter quite a particular relationship at sea, especially as a passenger in steerage. If, on the one hand, you save considerably by choosing this accommodation rather than the expensive cabin, then on the other hand you are also subject to many instances of unpleasantness. However, a not insignificant advantage remains for the passenger in steerage, since in the case of gales he does not feel the rolling motion of the ship as much as those in the cabin; for this reason the cabin passengers often joined us. Still, this advantage may be the only one granted steerage. When it comes to social interaction, a person with some claim to being educated will find more gratification in the cabin. In steerage it is, in effect, an annoying situation often to be restricted to individuals totally void of intellectual culture. It is even sadder when you are so unfortunate as to have to live with individuals from whom, judging by their education and social standing, you had expected better manners, but who learn from those others how to discard all decent behavior right away. They even practice how to become better at it, partly because of wickedness and chicanery, and find merit in outdoing the initial perpetrators when it comes to bad manners and vulgar conduct. When on top of this there is also gossip, tippling, and immoderate indulgence, then steerage assumes a veritable village mentality, and a wolf's lair is an Eden by comparison. In this description I don't believe I have exaggerated anything, as far as individual instances are concerned. The only remedy for a peace-loving man whose demon has led him to such a cave of savages is to approach his travel companions with the greatest of caution and to restrain himself altogether from any comments about them; it is unbelievable how quickly a merely casual remark spreads from one end of the ship to the other like a brush fire, and how much more untruth is added on in the process. On such voyages you all too often fall into the company of empty minds, and because of the utter idleness on board, such individuals know of nothing else to do except to have it in for their dear companions. As a consolation for the emigrant who may be frightened by this perhaps rather harsh description, I shall add, however, that the picture just presented of some version of Purgatory may occur to such a degree only rarely—and I want to wish from my heart that this will be the case for my dear countrymen. Moreover, much of this evil can be removed by keeping a demeanor as detached and conventional as possible. If, on the other hand, you are lucky enough to have good people with better manners for companions, then the voyage, all monotony notwithstanding, will provide much pleasure, and once your destination is reached, you often truly part with sadness.

It is now time for me to call my reader's attention to what items to take along for the voyage. Most likely, the majority of readers from the Weser area already know that passage, including board, from Bremen to New York amounts to forty Reichsthaler in gold; however, I negotiated for 37½ Reichsthaler, since I was not dealing with an agent, but directly with the shipping firm. That you must provide your own bedding will also only require passing mention, but it might not be unwarranted to advise against bringing heavy featherbeds. It is best to sell these at home, since those leaving for Texas, eastern Florida, or Louisiana should only bring bedding for their travel needs, filled with sea grass. Since, depending on the time of year, it may still occasionally be cold on this voyage, care should be taken at the least that you have comfortable and warm cover. For bedding needed at the end of the journey, it is practical merely to bring the covers; here and in those other countries, so-called Spanish hanging moss is found in abundance and provides very good fill. Not only is it healthier in this warm climate, but in this way you also save a good deal on freight.

Even though, as mentioned, free board is included for the forty Reichsthaler, you still have to provide dishes and plates, as well as teacups, coffee pots, etc.; nor should some tallow candles and a lamp as well as oil be omitted, since at least on some ships light is not provided in steerage. It is best to take pots and pans of tin or sheet metal, since earthenware vessels always break on the way from the movements of the ship. Right after seasickness is overcome, almost all passengers will find that salt meat does not agree with them; it is therefore a good idea to provide the following items: ham, some cheese, some good herrings, some wheat flour, some vinegar, some brandy and wine, some rather hard-baked loaves of rye bread, some syrup, tea, coffee, etc. Some of these items, at least on certain ships, you can have delivered, if—not this!—not too many passengers are present, but only by request, and often the quality is very poor. Therefore I cannot but rather strongly advise that these items be acquired, all the more so since on the other voyages you are responsible for your own provisions and can thus still use what is left over. I have still to advise those immigrants who, like myself, might decide to go to Texas that if the passage offered them in Bremen is far too expensive, then it is better to go directly to New Orleans than to make the detour by way of New York, or even Baltimore or Charleston. To be sure, I got off about four dollars cheaper going by way of New York than if I had gone directly to New Orleans; however, I was en route a good deal longer. In those immense cities in between, where there are so many occasions to spend money—and it is really not cheap there—many families might spend proportionately more than I had need to. In Bremen I was asked sixty Reichsthaler for freight, passage, and board direct to New Orleans. Least of all would I advise going to Baltimore or Charleston, since there is far less opportunity to travel to New Orleans from those places than from New York. There you find transportation in any week on some packet boat for ten dollars and your own provisions.

In bringing money, the so-called Spanish dollar or piaster should be chosen. I must advise my countrymen from the Weser coast that if they have some leisure time before embarkation, they should exchange their money for these coins in small sums. In the Oldenburg lands they may be had for one Reichsthaler in gold and eight Grote, whereas in Bremen they cannot be obtained for less than one Reichsthaler and twenty-four Grote; this rate is caused by the heavy demand from emigrants who leave by way of Bremen. If you have the opportunity to obtain securities from the Bank of the United States, then this would be a great advantage, provided the rate is not too high. They will gain, at least in many places in America, 5 percent over silver. One must merely be careful not to obtain bills or paper money from the many private banks operating in America, since these are not easy to negotiate. I thought I had already given necessary hints for everything to be procured, but looking now at this subject more closely, I cannot help but make one small addition. The gentle reader will kindly forgive me for this deviation from orderly procedure—in dealing with a multitude of subjects, and even after proper checking, the author does not always get everything included; some things only occur to you later, and thus there will be instances where I shall have to ask the reader's indulgence. I ask that you will really take to heart that you take as complete a provision as at all possible of all items of clothing and, if possible, of footwear, because all such items are quite monstrously expensive in America, and especially here in Texas. If you have a surplus of such items upon arrival, then they can be disposed of advantageously in return for necessary cattle and other such commodities. Although a mild climate prevails here and wintertime causes but little discomfort, still when a sudden north wind sets in during that season, the air will turn in a flash from being sunny and warm to a quite considerable cold. I must therefore advise everybody not to forget some woolen underwear; this will be all the more necessary since a warm, mild climate makes you more sensitive to the effects of the cold. Even though people wear their shoes without socks almost as a common practice, nevertheless on such days woolen socks will certainly not be an unwelcome item. If anyone should have forgotten one thing or another, do not forget to replenish in New York or New Orleans, preferably the former, for in this country prices are far higher. Thus in Brazoria a pair of shoes are 2½ dollars, but can be had in New York or New Orleans for 1 to 1¾ dollars. Depending on conditions, so it is with other items as well. Short, light cotton vests, all white or at least of light-colored material, and sturdy linen trousers for work are very welcome here, as well as a good supply of shirts, which people here do show off the most. In conclusion I must still add for the benefit of friends of the noble smoking tobacco that here it is provided by nature, so that everybody, with only slight effort, not only is able to grow the finest varieties for his own need but also finds his efforts amply rewarded by selling it, especially if it has been made into cigars. But the emigrant should not leave his dear German pipe at home, nor even several of them at that, since they can be sold to the Americans at great advantage. There is no shortage of stems, since a reed growing here can be used for those, but mouthpieces with tips suitable for these stems should not be forgotten. A small supply of all kinds of local garden seeds would also be very desirable here, as well as seeds of raspberries, red currants, or gooseberries; also seeds of strawberries, which are not found here, would be very welcome. As for flower seeds, everybody will have to select the varieties of which he is especially fond.

Now I may be allowed to resume the thread of my travel account. Truly I would now be able to entertain my worthy readers with a description of many sea animals, except for whales, as well as the phosphorescence of the sea and other such curiosities, but I fear I should be boring them, since in all travel accounts there is plenty of mention of such objects. Our *Leontine* was actually reminiscent of a kneading trough, for we only progressed at a snail's pace. I have admittedly been able to comprehend very little of navigation, but it seems to me that our German sailors do not know how to utilize every favorable little breeze like the Americans, whose swifter sailing must be due in good measure to the more pointed and practical design of their ships. It was already the second half of February, and still the land we had been anxiously looking forward to for so long did not want to make an appearance. One evening at this time an indescribably beautiful sight presented itself before us. The setting sun colored the many small clouds with all hues, from the brightest yellow to the darkest red, purple, and blackish-gray, and afterward I saw such a beautiful sky. At the same time, way down on the horizon a dense band of mist moved before us, announcing the proximity of land. The following morning this mist gave way to mountains, and little by little you could recognize rocks, bushes, and finally towers and houses. We soon came close to a rock called Block Island and saw to the left a long stretch of land with a lighthouse at the point [Montauk Point]; this was Long Island, which extends for eighty nautical miles before New York Bay. Since the wind was completely adverse, we were tacking along this island, several times coming face to face with it and just as often heading back out into the ocean. Finally, on the afternoon of February 19, the wind turned, and by the dark of evening we reached the mouth of the bay. Though we could now see several lighthouses, the captain did not find it advisable to enter, since we still did not have the eagerly awaited pilot on board. Thus the sails were turned, one against the other, so that we stayed in one location. We remained in this state until noon, when the pilot finally arrived. He was a vigorous young man with enormous whiskers extending down both sides of his face like an alley of linden trees; he was altogether a gentleman as well, and it really would have produced a sharp contrast if he had been put opposite a conventional German pilot as a counterpart. Being a genuine American, he used few words after having shaken the captain's hand; instead he went right to his post, taking the helm without eating the dinner offered him, and began to issue orders so forcefully and quickly that the sailors, not accustomed to such swift maneuvering, almost did not get hold of themselves. Upon questioning, the pilot surprised us with the pleasant news that health conditions in New Orleans were now good, according to the latest information. With regard to this subject I must add, in retrospect, that shortly before our departure from Bremerhaven we had read in the paper that in New Orleans cold plague along with yellow fever were raging, as well as cholera. He also produced several New York newspapers, from which we learned that the French and the Belgians had taken the citadel in Antwerp. After the pilot's long boat had rowed away, a gentleman came aboard who was delivering papers for several New York newspaper offices. It was a cold, clear winter day, and he pointed out a panorama to us, which I still think of with pleasure. All around we saw mountains, valleys, and the mouths of bays and rivers, with sailing ships scattered all over. The shores, adorned with villages and shrubbery, and the neat white houses provided an exceedingly pleasant view after we had seen nothing but sky and water for so long. Before us were two high mountain ridges, like the *Porta Westphalica* [Westphalian Gap]; sea passed between them. On one of them there was, to the left, a small village and a fortification with a telegraph; opposite from it and to the right was another fortification and, with water washing around its base, the recently erected Fort Lafayette. In the distance we saw mountains; to the left, behind the telegraph, were several islands ornamented with white villas and country houses—among them the high-lying Quarantine Island with its little cluster of houses was particularly noticeable. There was still nothing of New York to be seen, because the city is located on the right, farther into the bay or basin. On this day we were not granted the pleasure of seeing the destination of our long voyage, so almost all of us in steerage lay down fairly early in our berths. But when I opened my eyes the next morning, one passenger—who even under more ordinary circumstances would break into fairly exalted joy over every object and then express himself quite loudly—came tumbling into steerage with loud exclamation of the greatest amazement—one of the slippers grown dear to him coming off in the process—assailing us to follow him on deck immediately, since the whole city now lay before us. I must gladly confess, though, that this view was not very suitable for getting me up, for there was little more to be seen of the city than a few streets where lamps, close to going out, were still burning. Somewhat annoyed over having been disturbed from my rest, I went back to bed. However, when I went on deck in full daylight a few hours later, I was pleasantly surprised. In spite of the winter cold I had felt the previous day, the mildest, loveliest spring air was blowing toward me; the sun had just risen and was shining most charmingly on the splendid shores of the harbor. Before us we saw nothing but houses, and in front of them a forest of ships' masts, which did not allow anything to be distinctly recognized except the towers projecting above them, of which I counted sixteen just on this side. Even now several ministering spirits reported in with offers of this or that kind of assistance. We detached one of our fellow passengers to be under the wing of one of these spirits to fetch us something spirituous as well as some fresh bread, which we also coveted. Even though the greatest harmony had not always prevailed among us in steerage during the sixty-day voyage, still the joy of having the long trip safely behind us, along with the heartwarming drops in the bottle, turned us into a single great harmony, so great indeed that all morning long it did not even occur to us to go ashore. After having eaten, however, we could no longer resist the urging of our hearts. I am not able to describe with what feelings I set foot on American soil. How light I felt, and how comfortable, and how I did silently thank the Almighty that he had guided me safely and without accidents across the boundless Atlantic Ocean. But I sorely missed all my loved ones in the distant fatherland; how often I thought of my children, of my wife, how they would have enjoyed everything with me.

As I was walking through some street with a travel companion, we heard several salvos of fire from small rifles; we approached the area where the noise came from and found a detachment of the city guard in front of City Hall, firing these salvos in honor of the great Washington, whose birthday celebration took place on this day. From here the guard marched through several streets and we followed; they finally stopped on a public square, and the firing began again, this time by platoon. The uniforms and deportment of the guardsmen were fine, but their salvos crackled a lot, and I must say that the Hamburg Citizens' Guard surpasses them in precision firing. We still spent this night on board and did not leave the ship until the following afternoon. Although I had decided, for many reasons, to take lodging by myself in New York, still it was strongly urged upon me to rent a room with four former travel companions and likewise to set up an arrangement for joint housekeeping. Only the financial aspect prompted me to accept this proposal for the time being, as I reserved the right to separate again from the company according to how circumstances developed. So this morning I went with Mr. Schwarting, who has been mentioned several times, into the city to rent a room, which we finally achieved around noon after getting pretty tired from walking. It was from a German innkeeper by the name of Carl Schmidt, in Spruce Street [Charles F. Smith, 16 Spruce Street], for one dollar per week. In the rather spacious room there was also a fireplace that could be used for cooking. Mr. Schmidt treated us very well as time went on, and I highly recommend this upstanding man to other arriving friends and countrymen. He also has a so-called Bording [boarding] house, or eating and lodging quarters; for those who wish to use it, the price for lodging and full board is three dollars per week. Everything there is assuredly as good as may be found anywhere in New York where such a business is conducted, provided, that is, the price is the same. American breakfast, which is taken around eight o'clock, consists, as a rule, of several kinds of fried meat, sausages, boiled eggs, and good strong coffee. The season permitting, cress and lettuce are also served. Only white bread is put on the table, and as fine as might be found in Germany.

The experience of bringing our things ashore prompts me to advise later immigrants, if they have considerable supplies of new items of clothing, shoes, etc., to pack those in between their used things while they are still on board, since they may otherwise be considered trade items, which are subject to quite a high tariff, or even contraband. However, this is easily done, and often one friend can help another get something through. But on the whole, as long as you are careful not to arouse any suspicion, new immigrants are not checked very closely.

After we had taken our belongings to our new lodging in the afternoon, our joint household economy was established. The first item was to set up a community fund. This was done by having each *praenumerando* person deposit half a dollar, paid in advance; then we appointed an accountant, who also served as cashier. With this great achievement completed, we all went into the city to do our shopping. We arrived at an enormous market; in addition to meat, we found wild and domestic poultry there, and game ranging from squirrel and hare—or small gray rabbits—to bear and deer, and in the most pleasing selection. The buyers also stock all possible varieties of vegetables in greatest abundance. Here, at the end of February, we already found young green peas, cress, lettuce, etc. The prices of all the necessities of life on display here, of meat in particular, cannot be considered high. I was surprised to find meat cheaper here than in Hamburg. We found only fuel, which here consists largely of wood and coal, to be rather expensive.

New York, the largest and most populous mercantile city in North America, is located at the mouth of the Hudson, which

forms a wide basin two nautical miles wide and with a very romantic setting. In addition to the two fortifications already mentioned, there are four more for the protection of the city, which has
become a second Gibraltar. The city has approximately 230,000–
236,000 inhabitants; I have not been able to establish the exact population figure. In the meantime it continues to increase quite considerably. Nor was I able to determine the exact number of houses.
Some streets, which are straight as an arrow, have close to seven
hundred house numbers and are thus by themselves as big as the
city of Oldenburg. There are 152 [125] churches, some with beautiful towers. Some houses are solid brick, which are largely not
plastered here, but only given a still more beautiful red color and
mortared white. Some houses are built of wood and have rather a
friendly appearance. All houses are roofed with shingles of either
wood or tile—the former painted the color of the latter. However,
as far as these roofs in particular are concerned, I cannot say that
I like them; not to mention that they are by no means fireproof.
Apart from the black people, who constitute the servant class here,
a stranger is struck by nothing unusual, but imagines himself to be
in a German or a similar Dutch city. Dress and deportment are just
like at home. For its communication with surrounding cities and
regions, the city has fifty-one steamships [lines of packets] on regular runs; there is a recently built one here that traverses 150 English miles in nine hours, or as far as from Oldenburg to the Rhine
River, in this short span of time; the fare is only 1½ dollars. As the
reader will remember from Ernst's letter, a dollar is one hundred
cents or Grote. From here to Philadelphia, ninety-nine [eighty-
nine] miles, the fare is 1¼ dollars; this is traveled in twelve hours.
Included in this is a thirty-six-mile stretch by coach from New
Brunswick to the Delaware River; there you locate another steamer. Overland transportation is handled by sixteen coaches of four
with nine seats. Moreover, another two steamships with similar
connections leave daily for Philadelphia, and many more for other
distant cities; from Philadelphia, travel proceeds in the prescribed
manner to Baltimore. For local communication in the streets of
New York, there are—in addition to hundreds of [two hundred]

carriages for hire (*fiacres*), which are always in attendance in the streets and at the harbor—a number [eighty] of mobile dispatchers [city stages] constantly driving up and down the same street; but then again, some streets are an hour's journey long. The most important streets are illuminated by gas; here the stores for the most part are prosperous and large. Here I must make the observation, however, that in Hamburg, which is so distinguished in many ways, displays are often larger and in better taste. Since the city is surrounded by water on all sides and connected with the mainland only by a narrow strip, there are thousands of ships all around the city, from all nations and regions of the world; on an average, three thousand ships are said to arrive annually. The size of the city can be gathered from the fact that according to the city directory, there are 556 residents [555 entries] by the name of Schmidt [Smith]. Fourteen [twelve] different newspapers are published daily, some of sixteen sheets in size and very closely printed, as well as several periodicals. Almost every house has its store or shop where something is offered for sale, since everything is aimed at commerce. In the last ten years the city has increased so much that where the city hall is now located (a splendid palace, built entirely of white and red marble), which is approximately in its center, there was until recently a forest used for hunting; only a few sycamores have been left standing in any regular fashion. In recent years the annual customs levied amounted to about twenty million dollars.

Because of the many wooden houses there are fires here almost daily. Often my sleep was interrupted by fire bells. The local inhabitants are already used to this and do not worry about it; instead, when they wake up, they reach out and check the wall. As long as it is not hot, they are not likely to get up. The fire departments, however, are also so good that it is rare for more than one house to be burned down.

All denominations here enjoy free exercise of religious practice; even Anabaptists are found here. As in England, Sunday is entirely devoted to divine service; neither dancing nor working is permitted, and thus it is in all of the United States, except for New Orleans.

Tobacco is only smoked in the form of cigars here. Even when a German used to his little pipe does find some packaged tobacco, it is bad and expensive. You can easily get by with what is left over from cigars, however, and it is inexpensive and good.

The village of Broklyn [Brooklyn] is situated directly across from New York, on Long Island. As seen from the city it presents an attractive view, up high on an elevation, and with its pines and other trees and shrubbery, as well as country houses and mansions in between, it offers an indescribably friendly aspect. It has fifteen thousand inhabitants, many churches, and six [three] steamships, crossing from various streets to New York every five [ten] minutes. The Navy Yard is located here, harboring several ships of the line and frigates. Two of them are housed in their own specially built structures. In part the village lies between high sandhills; one of them has the most splendid view of New York and faces Williamsburg on the other side. The diversity of interesting scenes to be viewed from these heights would terrify the boldest painter, were he to venture sketching a picture. Brooklyn has the advantage of an exceptionally healthy location, and there may hardly be a place in the United States exceeding it in this respect; for this reason the population has been increasing so astonishingly that in one year it grew by five thousand souls. This place would long ago have deserved the name of "city," since it may be difficult to find a "village" of such size and population anywhere in the world. Still, the inhabitants are content with that modest name for their community, all the more since it exempts it from the greater city vices.

New York is situated below the 41st° northern latitude and thus on a line with Rome; it is very hot in summer, and even in January it is occasionally warm enough for perspiration to come to your face at table, and it becomes necessary to close the stores. Still, a very considerable cold may sometimes suddenly set in. Thus, as I noted earlier, during the first days of my stay here we had the most beautiful spring weather, although you could feel the cold evenings and nights; but after the course of five or six days a winter storm suddenly arrived and an enormous amount of snow fell, so that I was by no means missing or looking back to winter in my fatherland in northernmost Germany; on the contrary, I discovered it here in its harshest form. Here they usually have the beautiful fall weather in December that we are used to having in September in Germany. As a rule, spring begins in February; however, night frost does a good deal of damage later than that. Because of the proximity to the ocean, in the summertime they quite often have many instances of fog, but such is not the case farther inland. Conventional summer attire here consists of white vests and trousers, or white waistcoats with black silk kerchiefs; even the most distinguished dress in that manner this time of year.

All artisans earn substantial money here; thus a mason or a carpenter earns three dollars a day. They only work during daytime hours. Tailors, shoemakers, bakers, painters, etc., also make abundant wages. However, every newcomer should be advised for the present to be instructed in the English language, since he will otherwise get into embarrassing situations here. While I was here many German artisans complained a great deal about lack of work, for which the enormous pressure of immigrants may be to blame. It is claimed that this past year close to forty thousand Europeans came to New York. Whether this figure is quite reliable, I do not venture to decide, but it does not seem unbelievable to me, since I heard it of an old customs official who had to watch out for all German ships arriving and had easy access to all passenger lists, thus also those from other ships arriving. German artisans who do not find work immediately upon arrival in New York are perhaps better off going to Philadelphia right away, since more Germans live there.

In view of the enormous territory owned by the United States and not in cultivation, enough, perhaps, to have room for all of Europe—I need only call the Missouri region to mind—it cannot but hold true that a wide field of advancement is available to farmers. Even now the United States already supplies a third of the world's grain, and still there is a shortage of stirring hands to work the extremely fertile soil. So it is natural that farmers must be quite comfortable in this country; here the farmer is king, and the king becomes a farmer (I have in mind the farmer Joseph Bonaparte, former king of Spain, who until recently was still engaged in agriculture at Bordenton [Bordentown, New Jersey], on the Delaware). However, the farmer is by no means such a hounded animal as we are used to, where, at least in many countries, he is barely able to have enough left over to cover his taxes. Beyond a few dollars in local taxes for churches and schools, there are only slight fees and taxes; most of the expenditures of the entire country are defrayed by customs, mail service, and the sale of uncultivated land. The farmer does not have to strain his land with a great deal of fertilizer to grow his products, and with its abundance the soil is so loose that it only requires a light plow, which he can carry on his shoulder. Cattle are so hardened here that they are never sheltered, except perhaps for milking; often calves are born in the snow. They are all chased off into the woods, find their own feed, and find their way home again; even in New York, hogs and cows run loose in the streets, which admittedly runs quite counter to the German notion of police regulation. It must sound just as wondrous to a German, when he first arrives, to hear dogs and every head of cattle addressed as "Sir." The main product is Turkish and conventional wheat. The latter has an octagonal stem and heads often a foot long, with a height of up to seven or eight feet. In addition, rye and other grains are raised. Everybody is free to hunt here; there are but few hares, but all the more deer, partridges, pheasants, guineas, and wild rabbits, which are gray here and look like young hares. There is also much other game and poultry, even bears—which, incidentally, are not mean—and in some areas, wolves as well. For Americans, hunting is a Sunday pastime; even at the age of ten, children are seen in the woods with their rifles. The many rivers have an abundance of fish, often quite large, and thus angling is very interesting. There is an astonishing quantity of oysters and quite large and fat ones; I saw some a foot long. You find your own at the shore.

The United States maintains a military force of only six thousand men, largely posted at the English border with Canada, to prevent illegal trade. Conscription is not known at all here; in case of war, everybody is a soldier, for which reason military exercises take place every summer.

It can, in fact, be stated that here a man is taken for what he is actually worth, since little or no distinction in social standing is practiced. Anybody enters the hotel of his liking, and nobody tips his hat to another man. If even the most distinguished man has been treated honestly and well by an ordinary workman and chances upon him in the street, he will cordially extend his hand and go with him to the nearest tavern and have a drink with him.

From here the arriving colonists either go south to the banks of the Ohio or west to the Great Lakes. The Ohio is indeed a few degrees closer to the Equator, but marketing of products is far more difficult there than in the other region mentioned, since everything must be shipped from the Ohio to the Mississippi and down that great river to New Orleans. On lakes Erie and Ontario, there is direct transport. On the Ohio, the price per acre used to be three dollars and five dollars at the lakes. An acre is forty poles or rods in length, and four in width. However, those prices are from a report now already several years old, so it is possible they might now be somewhat different; I must also note that they apply only to private holdings. All land to be had from the government is now set lower and is granted for 1¼ dollars; this is the so-called Congress Price throughout the United States of North America. It used to be 2½ [two] dollars. During the time span in question, colonists usually obtained fifty acres from land speculators for 250 dollars, which they did not have to pay, however, but mortgaged over twelve years at 6 percent; so they actually had to pay only fifteen dollars in lease money. You also buy land partly in cultivation from country people by paying them 1½ to 3 dollars more an acre; this earnest money was paid in ready cash and the balance mortgaged. The land is forested with beautiful trees of quite considerable height. Incidentally, the woods in this region are not as dense as we are used to, but rather have trees ten to twelve feet apart; even the oaks are slender and straight, without side branches, similar to our coniferous trees, but they are not thick and are cut with a few strokes. If a colonist has made a purchase, all the neighbors quickly gather with teams and equipment to build him a house. This is accomplished in two days and only costs him approximately two dollars for whiskey (corn liquor). It is a so-called log cabin of tree trunks for his initial needs, until he can build a more comfortable one later. In a similar manner, clearing an acre of woodland only costs one dollar in liquor. What a major undertaking building a house in Europe is by comparison, and how easy and inexpensive here. You build a ground floor of rocks (in many locations these are found in abundance in the field) and the upper one of wood. The beams are pine, three inches thick and about ten inches wide. The siding on the outer walls is planed and nailed at the bottom so that the one below is always covered like roofing tile. This style of building is quite presentable, particularly when narrow siding is used. With four hundred pieces of siding, which are very inexpensive hereabouts, you can build a neat little house in this manner. Nails are very cheap, only ten to twelve cents a pound, whether short or long; they are machine made. Since cattle are so little trouble, it is advantageous to buy a few head right away; they always find adequate feed on the land not in cultivation. Hogs multiply unbelievably here as well and are very fat. Old horses are not to be killed, but are chased off into the woods. The city of Buffalo is situated between lakes Erie and Ontario, three hours from the greatest natural wonder of the world, Niagara Falls. The city has risen extremely quickly and is already large and populous; everything is marketed there at good prices. The sale of firewood alone provides adequate trade there, but whoever can go easy on his woodlands for a few years will get good returns. The location of this city on the lakes makes for an exceedingly healthy and mild climate; it is in the state of New York, 450 miles (150 hours) from the city of the same name, nine degrees closer to the Equator than northern Germany, and thus on a line with the Tyrol and upper Italy. It is reached from New York by steamship on the Hudson River as far as Albany, and from there on canals, in six days. Colonists immigrating in this area must at least bring enough money to defray initial equipment, for which 200–250 Reichsthaler will be required. Those with a desire to operate an inn can profitably open a public house near the city. The region described does indeed have many advantages, and the writer of the letter at the beginning of this book, Mr. Ernst, was already of a mind to settle there when he read [Gottfried] Duden's book about Missouri. That area appealed more to him, and together with a German friend, Mr. Fordtram [Charles Fordtran], he was already on his way to New Orleans, and from there to Missouri, when through a fellow passenger on his way to Texas he came across a printed description of this country; this immediately prompted him and his friend to make Texas their unconditional preference. And certainly, the two friends had the best-founded reasons to prefer the splendid land of Texas, which of all American states opens the most splendid prospect for the agriculturist; for in comparison to those countries it has almost no winter, and in the summertime the constant refreshing breeze cools the air so much that as a result it is hardly as warm as there—not to mention many other important advantages. Nobody in the United States is better off than the women; at least on average they do not work much, and even of female domestics only woman-like work can be expected. When you see a farmer's wife go to town in her small, elegant one-horse carriage, you imagine you are seeing a lady of high estate; even the husband is quite a gentleman in such a situation. Servants' wages are quite high here; a kitchen maid, for example, earns ten to twelve dollars a month and for that does kitchen work exclusively. Consequently, people of more modest means must often forgo such help, since, apart from blacks, it is also quite scarce. In the city of New York there are quite good schools, in which the young people make good progress very quickly.

Now may I be allowed to give the reader a list of all the United States. They are: 1. Maine; 2. Vermont; Newhamptonschire [New Hampshire]; Massachuset [Massachusetts]; 5. New York; 6. Pennsylvania; 7. New Jers[e]y; 8. Ohio; 9. Mariland [Maryland]; 10. Rhode-Islad [Rhode Island]; 11. Michigan (Territory); 12. Indiana;

13. Kentucky; 14. Tennesse[e]; 15. North Carolina; 16. South Carolina; 17. Georgia; 18. Alabama; 19. Florida; 20. Missis[s]ippi; 21. Louisiana; 22. Arkansas (Territory); 23. Illenois [Illinois]; 24. Missouri; 25. Connecticut; 26; the large Missouri Territory, which, by itself alone, could constitute an empire. As readers can tell by looking at the map, some states are of quite a considerable size. It is cause for wonder that this enormous free country is governed with so little expenditure and so few officials, and that attention is still given to everything concerning the good of the whole. But Americans do avoid all verbal expansiveness; accustomed to dealing with everything in brevity, they do not allow time for unnecessary formalities. Communication by water is quite excellent in the United States. When going to one of the more important places, you look for the cheapest and fastest transportation.

On the whole, Americans are less given to amusement than we are. There is not much playing at cards, more Dominos; bowling I have never heard of, though there are a few alleys in New York. Generally there is more work than play, and popular amusements such as balls and dance parties are quite rare here. When it comes to community or group singing, Americans are also quite behind; their popular tunes actually sound barbarous. There are several theaters, decorated most splendidly. [*William*] *Tell* and [*Der*] *Freischütz* have often been given with great success.

Those applying for citizenship of the United States must solemnly disavow their former sovereigns, and after three years they obtain their certificates for five Reichsthaler. Items of clothing are expensive here, because of the wages of the makers; they are made by hand, and where no machines can be used, things are expensive. For example, a pair of ordinary children's stockings is twenty-four to thirty-six cents; linen is also very expensive, so generally you use cotton cambric.

In America, children are a great treasure. The more children you have, the more welcome you are. If they want to learn a trade, they are apprenticed early. From the beginning, they receive a four-dollar wage per month, with board, and are apprentices until the age of twenty-one, when they become masters right away. It must be presumed that even in instances of only average ability, no bunglers are produced by this system. So those who bring a lot of boys along and board them at home, for which, incidentally, the master pays compensation of four dollars a month, can perhaps even live frugally on this alone.

Now it is time to say a few words about Pennsylvania, this first refuge of Germans in America; even now they are still in a majority. The land here is very fertile and was some years ago still very inexpensive—an acre could be had for four to five dollars, of which 3–3½ was mortgaged. The climate is healthful. Here, as in several states, farmers have a sideline in sugar manufacture from sugar maples, which grow in abundance. Wheat weighs seventy pounds per bushel here. Here, too, farmers do very well; a market for their

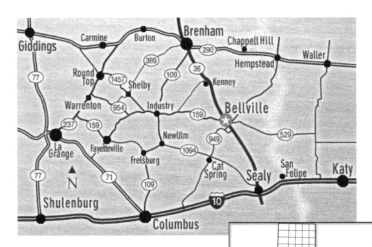

Figure 7. A map of Industry, Frelsburg, Cat Spring, and Columbus. The *Sabine* with Jordt on board entered the Brazos River by Velasco on or about April 28, 1833. After much delay Jordt arrived in San Felipe around June 30, 1833.

products is assured by the many rivers, and in good years they can usually make enough to pay out their land. For the purchase of a place of about fifty acres, no security is required anywhere. If you cannot pay the interest—on fifty acres, it is 10–12½ dollars—you must vacate. On the whole, Americans are not at all suspicious.

After this little digression, permit me to return to New York. The interiors of local churches are exceptionally beautiful. They are spacious, elegant, and very neat. A number of stoves spread very pleasant heat, and the comfort you feel while there is no doubt conducive to church visitation.

I want to close this chapter with a few hints about how immigrants who go by way of New York might manage to set up with the least expense. It goes without saying that all German countrymen who travel south or to Texas from here do best by shortening their stay in New York as much as possible; since they will, however, rarely get away in less than a week, it will be practical at any rate to inquire with the captain about the possibility of occupying your former shipboard lodging for this length of time. This will rarely be refused by a reasonable captain, if that very space is not to be used immediately for taking on new freight. If this is agreed to and concern for lodging thus overcome, there is no cheaper place to go for dinner than at an eating-house or a basement diner; here the food is even cheaper and better than in the boardinghouses mentioned above. In the mornings and evenings anybody can easily get by with buttered bread and tea or coffee. These basement taverns are usually found near market squares.

DEPARTURE FROM NEW YORK
FOR NEW ORLEANS.

Description of This City.
Observation on the Most Essential Needs
of the Colonist in Texas.

ON THE FIRST OF MARCH Mr. S. [Schwarting], who has been mentioned several times, and I left New York on the packet boat *Illinois*. Our landlord up to that time, Mr. Schmidt, had been so obliging as even to assist us with the purchase of provisions for the trip. We had spent nine dollars on this purchase and had obtained so much for this amount that even my half share was sufficient for me until New Orleans and Brazoria, with very little supplement needed. An immigrant to Texas will do well to procure his supply of coffee and sugar in New York, since these items are more expensive in New Orleans and higher still in the Texas towns he will be passing through. However, a small supply of some two hundred pounds of wheat flour can be had cheaper in New Orleans than in the former city. When it comes to items of this nature, and also whiskey (corn liquor), whatever you may carry in excess of personal need can be marketed in Texas at considerable advantage; whiskey is particularly high here, there being no distilleries as yet in the entire country. It might be said in passing that establishing one would certainly be very advantageous, the Americans being very fond of this drink.

For this trip we had once again chosen steerage. It is truly amazing that for a trip this considerable, the fare is only ten dollars.

Once again we were lucky enough to share our quarters with only nine persons, all of them decent people, and moreover had the pleasure of a larger space than on the Bremen ship, the *Illinois* being a good deal larger than the *Leontine*. A raw and chilly winter wind was blowing hard as we took leave of the pleasant city of New York; the entire rigging was covered with ice, as was the deck. Pleased though I was about approaching a milder climate, I was still somewhat saddened to see winter depart. Since I was fairly certain that I might never again in my lifetime witness such a European configuration of this season, I remembered all the more vividly the many winter pleasures we had enjoyed back in the beloved fatherland. No one will take offense at my claim that even the raw winter season has its pleasant aspects which should not be dismissed. I now vividly projected myself back to the time of my happy youth—when an ice-skating party was one of my greatest delights, and when I later made cross-country sled excursions with dear friends, how it felt when we returned to be greeted by a warm stove and a cozy little room; or I would recall those snowstorms when I defied the wild weather with a book in my hand. To be sure, I might also contrast those pleasant memories with a trip I once made in the severest cold I have ever experienced, when I had to struggle with all of the hardships of a cold climate; however, we humans seem to be so constituted that once something unpleasant is behind us, just having prevailed is satisfaction enough, whereas pleasant experiences persist longer in our memory, and lucky are the persons who remember only these. Now, to return to our journey, I must observe that just as in the case of Mr. Ernst, only four days after our departure the mild breezes of spring were blowing in our direction, and that a few days later, between Cuba and Florida, we had veritable summer. The weather being warmer now, I especially enjoyed the lovely evenings; we would often spend half the night sitting on deck. After about sixteen days, we finally reached the mouth of the Mississippi. Not far from there a pilot had already come aboard. Where this enormous river empties into the ocean, there is cane growing along both banks and an enormous amount of driftwood has piled up here. Still, the width of the river is not as considerable as I had expected; in this respect, it is exceeded by far by the mouths of both the Elbe and the Weser. Still, this lesser width affords the traveler the advantage of being able to view the houses of the agreeable plantations in a quite leisurely manner. Since it is upstream all the way, a steamship was engaged; it was already towing a three-master, which then came between the steamer and our ship. The noise of the engine works in the steamboat, sounding like distant cannon and following a regular beat, did stun me somewhat at first, but little by little your ear got used to it; my ship companions, who at first found this barbarous music very disagreeable, also got to be more indifferent about it. The following morning when I got on deck fairly early, I was most pleasantly surprised. On both sides of the gently flowing river I could see the neatest country houses, hidden away in stands of oranges that adorned the surrounding gardens and right next to large plantings of sugarcane; the distance was enclosed by an impenetrable primeval forest extending on both sides of the Mississippi as far as the eye could follow; it gives the traveler an approximate notion of the enormous forest holdings of America. All the shrubs and bushes were already displaying the tenderest green, and it made me feel uncommonly good to be greeted, as it were, by the month of May as early as March. Here the thought took vigorous hold of me that man is not tied to one little spot on earth, and that the beautiful world that God has made has such an abundance of areas and regions where we can prevail, and that it is often because of cowardice, lack of resolve, and inertia that people continue to knead the same old sourdough, until finally the resources have vanished for seeking a new fatherland far away; and when they are finally roused from deep slumber and almost reduced to the status of beggars, despair often sets in.

The vicinity here at the bank is flat, as are the banks themselves. All the workers on these plantations are slaves; I felt sorry for the poor Negroes when I saw them being herded like cattle for work early in the morning. The huts that these unfortunate creatures inhabit contrasted sharply with the tasteful country houses of their lords and masters. Three days after the steamboat had reached us, at eleven o'clock in the morning, we could see the city of New Orleans in the distance. One certain fellow inhabitant of our steerage was maybe more elated about this view than anybody else. The poor man had been seasick almost the entire trip, at least when there was the slightest wind. His almost continuous discomfort pained me all the more, since I have almost never encountered a more humane travel companion. Finally, we reached the city around three o'clock in the afternoon, but we were not able to go ashore until almost evening since we were quite some distance from the wharf, and thus first had to be connected with planks before we could leave the ship. We had been underway from New York a total of nineteen days, which is the customary duration of a journey such as this; still, Mr. Ernst got across in eleven days, but that is a rare instance. It was a lovely summer evening when I finally had land underfoot, all the more striking since it was only the twentieth of March. I was wandering arm in arm with the travel companion just mentioned, Mr. Reatsch [Harvey Rich], an American mechanic who was accompanied by his wife and young son, as we roamed the streets of the harbor district. In his exuberance, the good man couldn't do enough for us. We went to a confectionery, where he bought oranges, etc.; in short, he was quite generous, and we didn't get back on board ship until about eleven o'clock. The following morning it was considerably cold; upon arrival here, you have to be prepared for this kind of weather change. After a bit of breakfast, I hurried back ashore again to look for lodging. After the sun was somewhat higher in the sky, I enjoyed a most lovely morning and with the greatest of pleasure walked the streets of this city, which, generally speaking, is not exactly beautiful, but quite affluent. By about noon I had finally achieved my purpose after doing a lot of running around and had found a suitable place to stay at the residence of a German; along with board, it was negotiated at 3½ dollars per week. When I came aboard again in the afternoon to fetch my things for my new lodging, I found Mr. Rich busy doing the same. We took leave in the most sincere manner, and I had to make him a promise to visit regularly during our stay in New Orleans. Just as you often find the least support for any enterprise in your own fatherland and the least amount of true friendship among so-called friends who only consider themselves such as long as fortune favors us—likewise the least feeling of kinsmanship among actual countrymen—this very thing was happening to me, too. It was far harder for me to part from this particular friend than from my own countrymen, and I could have had no higher desire than for him to go to Texas with me. But his further travel would take him instead to Mexico City, where he expected to make a considerable profit, his occupation having to do with the machinery for steamboats as well as other ingenious items of steel and brass; he had already accumulated a considerable fortune doing work of this nature in New York.

As my reader will already know, the city of New Orleans was established by the French. As mentioned, it can lay no claim to beauty since, strictly speaking, it only has two fine streets, Chartre [Chartres] and Royal. Though the city is built according to plan and concept, beautiful stone houses are constantly found directly next to wooden ones, which, moreover, have but a poor appearance. The place is in a swamp, as is the entire area, this making it exceedingly unhealthy, with yellow fever prevailing here every year from June to October; people of standing and affluence then flee to the country. There is a lot of money in circulation, tempting many workingmen from all parts of the United States to come here, wages being better than anywhere else. Since, as already stated, the city is of French origin, many people of that nationality live here, and so do many Spaniards. The laws in force under the earlier French government have been retained up to the present. Street names are indicated at corners, French on one side, English on the other. Except for flour, all food items are more expensive and are not as good in quality as in New York. As noted at the beginning of this chapter, the air here is quite variable; during my stay here, the warmest summer air would often prevail during the evenings, and when I chanced to wake up in the middle of the night, it would be cold enough for me to have to put on a woolen undershirt in order not to catch cold.

New Orleans commerce is very active, and very magnificent business establishments are found here. To me it was very amusing to see [Choctaw] Indians every day; these are the ones who have separated from their tribes, partly adopted European ways, and settled in a forested area [at Bayou Lacomb] near the city. They bring game to [the French] market, as well as little braided baskets, things made of furs, hides, reeds, etc.; they get drunk on what they take in, even to the extent of staggering about dreadfully in the streets, with the silliest jumps and gestures. Most of these Indians have a fairly thick layer of red makeup applied to their yellowish-brown faces. They are generally hardy and excitable individuals; even so, they dislike accommodating themselves to farming and any regular activity, preferring hunting and selling hides to all other activities. Sundays and holidays in the United States being admittedly too dead for a German, who is used to his Sunday pleasures, here in New Orleans, by comparison, they also make too little of the occasion. Almost all artisans work on Sunday mornings, and around the ships there is as much going on all day long as there is during the week; even street music may be heard. When it comes to public morality, there is not much to praise this city for. The police are not at all able to maintain proper law and order; burglaries occur every night, and murder and street robbery are commonplace. Although executions are frequently carried out here, they are by no means capable of keeping the abuses under control. During my stay here, there were burglaries in seven locations in one night, and almost every week murder victims were found in the street early in the morning. Dueling is common, even among civilians, and it is no rarity, especially among the French, for journeymen of the various trades to fight it out with swords and pistols. Some of the streets are very dirty, particularly the more remote ones; the stone pavement is sinking in the swampy ground. Cobblestones for paving are not found locally, but imported from New York. Almost all the servants and maids are Negro slaves. In some instances they are treated very badly, and to magnify the injustice toward these poor people even more, they are often given their freedom when they become old and incapable of working. In public squares, churches, etc., you encounter such unfortunate individuals all the time, beseeching the generosity of passersby, that being their only recourse left. In every weekly paper, sales of slaves are announced; it goes without saying that these are Negroes who have been in America for quite some time or were born here, since, as is well known, the importation of slaves is prohibited; nevertheless, some are reportedly still smuggled in. I have watched many an auction of such Negroes at the [*Bourse* or] Exchange, and always with a feeling of indignation; at such times, they were carefully groomed, their burning black eyes cast down in shame.

Steamship traffic is also quite active here; I saw steamboats of enormous size coming and going. They go up the Mississippi to the Ohio, to the state of Missouri, etc.

Next a list will follow of items particularly vital for the Texas immigrant, most of which can be procured at the place of business of Mr. Martienstein [John H. Martinstein], [13] rue de Bienville, in New Orleans; he is a German who, it is hoped, will give everybody the right kind of service; if a particular item might still be missing here and there, he will call attention to it.

List

1 heavy plow; 1 light plow; 2 ox chains; harrow teeth made of iron (these may be brought from Germany). 1 large crosscut saw; 1 broad handsaw; 1 hatchet; 2 good woodman's axes (in New Orleans); 1 pair of iron wedges for splitting wood; 1 hammer; 1 pair of nippers; 1 auger; various drill bits for making holes from ½ to 3 inches (in New Orleans); several cold chisels of varying sizes (in New Orleans); 1 wood chisel (likewise); nails of various sizes, particularly 1 inch, for nailing short boards on houses (in New Orleans); a few light chains for horse harnesses (from Germany; here anybody can make his own straps for these); some iron hoes for garden or field work; 1 spade (in New Orleans); 1 scythe blade, which could be brought from Germany; 1 rasp; 1 file; 1 iron pot

with fireproof cover for baking bread (in New Orleans); 1 pancake pan (from Germany); some shoe-repair materials; 1 large butcher knife; various kinds of rope; some tin milk pans (for Texas, these are better than the wooden ones—from Germany); 1 gun (better one with conventional flintlock than percussion. There is general complaint here about frequent misfiring); ammunition (as to shot, buckshot and birdshot should be brought). Some drums for wagon wheels, or so-called hub boxes of iron (here wheels usually are made of solid slabs sawed off from a tree). Some hoop irons for wagon axles and shafts. Some iron wire and a pair of pliers (from Germany). Flaxen twine (this item to be brought in quantity from Germany, since it is rarely found in America). Darning needles (here the same applies). Some patterns for male and female dress. 1 drawknife; some good coarse tote sacks (from Germany); some planes with wooden wedges (if these might be somewhat more expensive in New Orleans than in Germany, they are also considerably better). 1 trowel. 1 masonry hammer (from Germany). 1 carpenter's adze for hollowing out troughs (in New Orleans). 1 coarse grating iron for grating fresh corn. 1 round grindstone (from Germany). Some iron cowbells (to be brought along from Germany, as they are very expensive here). Fishing hooks of various sizes, along with lines (from Germany); 1 flour sifter (from Germany); 1 board or wood cleaver for splitting boards for house shingles (in New Orleans); 1 or several good horse blankets (from Germany), as well as a saddle (Spanish saddles can be bought in New Orleans for three dollars; they are more practical than the expensive English ones). Some of the more common medical supplies, such as emetics, rhubarb, Glauber's salt, Peruvian bark, quinine, etc., should also be brought from Germany, since such items are expensive here.

Some of the items noted here to be procured in New Orleans might well be somewhat cheaper in Germany; however, they are not as good there, and many of these items are neither known nor to be had in Germany.

TRAVEL FROM NEW ORLEANS
TO BRAZORIA IN TEXAS.

Staying There and at Varner's Creek;
Departure for San Felipe and Mill Creek.
Observations Concerning These Localities.

I HAD ALREADY STAYED in New Orleans for four weeks when I decided to travel on. Among the many Germans located here, I had the good fortune to get acquainted with many an honorable man who received me very well and showered me with friendship and kindness, for which I here publicly extend to them my most sincere and warmest thanks. Although Mr. Ernst in his letter proposes that one make the trip to Texas by way of Harrisburg, it was still not possible for me to do so, since during my entire stay here all the ships were bound for Brazoria instead; sometimes two ships would be leaving for this place within a week, but then it might be another two weeks before another one departed from there again, so I consequently advise my countrymen to use the first and best opportunity. The schooners bound for Texas are usually berthed in the vicinity of the customs house; for the information of travelers, these and all the other ships in port display small signs with their destinations indicated. The schooner *Sabine*, Captain [Jeremiah] Brown in charge, which I chose, already had forty passengers on board, whose luggage was crowding the hold and the deck so much that, since I came on board somewhat later, I did not find the most favorable place for my things; with quite a few others, I also shared the lot of having to sleep on deck almost every night. On a clear Sunday, April 22 [21], after we had been waiting for wind since Saturday afternoon, to my delight it finally came up about one o'clock in the afternoon and moved us downstream so swiftly that within a few days [hours] the city was no longer in sight. The following morning we were already at the mouth of the Mississippi and had barely reached open sea when, in a number of instances, the effects of seasickness began to set in; however, in my own case, I did not suffer at all, which was all the more noteworthy as I had after all spent four weeks ashore since my second voyage. Other than myself there were three other Germans aboard our schooner; two of them, coming from New York, were also intending to go to Mr. Ernst's in Austin's Colony. Little of note happened during this trip. We had clear weather all the way, many times almost calm, however, so that it took about one week before we were able to get to the mouth of the Brazos River. The morning of that very day, a strong wind came up, almost turning into a gale around two o'clock in the afternoon. Accompanied by terrible cursing from the captain, whose orders, as it seemed, were not being carried out promptly enough, we did, however, finally enter safely. The region of Texas at the mouth of the Brazos appears quite pleasant; the town and fort of Velasco is laid out here, but other than a salt works, the town has but few houses, since it has just recently been established. I cannot express how happy it made me feel finally to behold the land that was the destination of my long journey, and its friendly appearance could but enhance my delight. The wide, green expanse, interspersed with wooded areas, made an impression on me that was all the more pleasant, since the color of the bushes and woods and grass is so delicate this time of year that I had never seen the like. The clear Italic sky, of which we can form no idea in our part of the world, also increased my pleasure and filled me with thanks to the Almighty, who had safely guided me across such a distance.

As we got farther upstream, our progress was made very difficult by the many bends in the river. The ship often had to be tied

by a long rope to a tree on the bank, and it could only be made
to move ahead very slowly by the combined pulling of the entire
crew. Both banks of the river are covered with thick woods here
and they are fairly steep, or at least much more so than those of the
Mississippi. At this snail's pace, we could not help but suffer greatly
from boredom; finally, after one long week, we reached Brazoria. I
had indeed imagined this city to be quite different. I counted but
few houses, all of them wooden; but in America, this should surprise no one since, at least in the United States, cities just recently
laid out have been known to swell to ten thousand and more inhabitants in a matter of years.

The town site is set directly by the riverbanks on cleared woodland. It is to be hoped that under the free republic, Brazoria will
be able to thrive, something that was not at all possible under the
late Spanish government. At the time of my arrival, much rain had
fallen in the area, so that all country roads, especially in the vicinity of the town, had badly deteriorated. We were told that it would
be another twelve miles (here we speak strictly of English miles),
at Belleslending [Bell's Landing], before they were passable again;
there it should be possible to engage wagons. Since our captain
had to go up to this location, he promised us, upon request, to
take us as well as our belongings along free of charge, for which
reason we were compelled to stay here for another week, but during that time we stayed on the ship. Finally, it was time to move
on, but the river had swelled so much that we had to spend almost
as much time covering these twelve miles as from Velasco to Brazoria; moreover, the masts and rigging regularly became stuck in
the trees. Finally, after the most boring stretch of my entire journey, we reached the eagerly awaited Bell's Landing; it consists of
a mere four or five houses. In Brazoria one of the Germans, Mr.
[Bernard] Scherrer, had separated from us. He had heard about attractive areas on the Colorado and had in mind to explore them; at
a later time, at Mr. Ernst's, he would report the results of his trip
to me and his friend, a Mr. F., who was staying behind with me.
Accordingly, he left all his things with us. After Mr. F. and I had

to spend several days at Bell's Landing, since no boat was available for the further trip up to Warner's [Varner's] Creek, we prevailed upon Captain Brown to help us out. On this occasion I must warn my countrymen bound for Texas against making the crossing with this particular Captain B. Payment of ten dollars had been agreed to for fare and luggage from New Orleans to Brazoria, but now at our departure he still wanted to charge us separately for each item, letting only our bedding pass free. What were we to do, having neither a written contract nor witnesses. But since the amount did not, for any of us, exceed three dollars, we preferred to pay it to avoid delay and further unpleasantness in the matter. So I advise subsequent immigrants to make written freight arrangements for their things, whether on land or by sea. When our boat was finally loaded, we were very happy finally to be rid of the notorious *Sabine*; it may have been six o'clock in the evening when we had finally accomplished that much of our purpose. The creek we now turned into is heavily covered with shrubbery. A lovely and beautiful evening favored our progress. The creek snakes in all directions through wild shrubbery, which spreads pleasant coolness and turned our trip into a pleasant water party; however, we were not able to go as far as Varner's Creek this day and, after tying our boat to a tree, had to decide to camp for the night on water, wrapped in our horse blankets. The mosquitoes attacked us ferociously, so we got but little rest and thanked God for the graying of a new dawn, enabling us to continue on our journey. It might have been about eight o'clock when we arrived at a settlement that we took to be Varner's Creek, but we learned that we had to continue upstream for another half hour; still the good people were so hospitable and prevailed upon us to partake of their breakfast, which had just been served up. After our bad night, we were happy to oblige. The owner of this settlement, a Mr. [Morgan] Rector, was of German descent; during my subsequent three-week stay at Varner's Creek, I visited these kindhearted people several times and was always received in the same friendly manner. Mr. Rector used to say that German blood was still pulsing in his veins, and if being upright and honorable is still the mark of this in the year 1833, then he was perfectly right. As promised, after another half hour we arrived at Mr. [Martin] Varner's settlement. We were happy to encounter—as may be presumed from his name—still another man of German descent. The prairie,[4] which is crossed by the road to San Felipe, begins here on Varner's property. After a stay of several days at this settlement, a teamster promised us that as soon as his wagons returned from San Felipe, he would take our things there, but since the roads were still very bad in some places, our departure kept being delayed day after day. Wagons were now arriving daily from San Felipe, but we could not be conveyed by them, since they were not able to obtain their freight as promptly as we could have wished. Although this delay on the one hand was annoying to me, it may on the other hand have been very beneficial. What happened, after I had already suffered from abdominal pain and lack of appetite for several days, was that I contracted cold fever; however, after the first attack, it only returned three times and then bothered me no more. It was during this period of time that my countryman, F., was overcome by homesickness. Before this I had already noticed one characteristic about him, that he would make different plans all the time and then quickly drop them again; in short, that he was highly indecisive. Since he now unfortunately got the fever, his courage was quite broken; constantly vacillating, he was determined at one moment to pursue his travel plan, but would then immediately wish to do the opposite. One Sunday afternoon I was lying deep in sleep when he quickly roused me and hastily forced on me a sum of money entrusted to him by his above-mentioned friend, Mr. Scherrer, so I could take it to our destination, Mill Creek; likewise, he turned over to me all of his travel companion's belongings so that I could take everything, and he very briefly reported to me that he had now found an opportunity to go down to Brazoria, where a ship would be departing for New Orleans the following day. I must confess that I was actually more annoyed than saddened by his departure. In New York he had left his wife and child with her wealthy brother, who had already subsidized his travels and undertakings rather considerably. At the conclusion of his travels, F. could still count on all possible support; he had been sent out in advance just so that he could give a reliable account of conditions in Texas. If the available lands there agreed with his expectations, the brother-in-law would then—together with several affluent Germans—leave New York and go himself. But now all the travel money entrusted to F. was virtually wasted.

The lower Brazos is not the healthiest of regions, since it is subject at times to overflows; but only intermittent fever is prevalent there, along with a kind of bilious fever; the former is rarely persistent, and the latter is rarely dangerous.

The prairie, which begins at the Varner settlement, is fairly level. Among the plants here I even found our German blackberries, in enormous quantity and, though this was only in May, quite ripe. There are also quite a few mulberry trees, but no longer with ripe berries; these are picked as early as the middle of April, particularly by squirrels and wild turkeys. We also found many silkworms on these trees. What significant business prospects this might have if knowledgeable immigrants were to arrive. In these parts I also saw various kinds of wild grapes. It is to be hoped that viticulture may flourish in Texas a few years from now; several individuals from the Rhineland are speculating in this direction and giving thought to introducing cultivated varieties suitable for this climate. This branch of industry could occupy thousands and quickly make them wealthy, since wine is very expensive around here and, in view of the free constitution, production can never be burdened with oppressive taxes. Mr. Varner, with whom I was staying, also had sugarcane, which did particularly well. The peach trees that had been planted also grew splendidly and were heavy with fruit; they ripen as early as July. Finally, after I was fully restored again, the teamster I had engaged reported that everything was ready for San Felipe. I had him sign a paper binding him to deliver to my order in San Felipe one hundred pounds of freight in good condition for 1½ dollars. We set out with seven wagons, each drawn by six oxen. The road was very good and I was exuberant, after waiting for three long weeks, finally to get moving from the same spot. Toward noon we stopped by a spring winding its way through a wild and beautiful valley covered with shrubbery. I had kept walking slowly ahead on the straight road, since the ox wagon was far too slow for me. After I had rested under a shade tree and restored myself *à la Diogenes* with a refreshing drink from the spring, the wagon train did finally arrive. Some people started a fire right away, others fetched water, while still others were busy untying the oxen, which hurried to the spring as soon as they were free of their yokes. Now there was a lot of activity, coffee and pancakes were made, etc. I may fairly claim that nothing had ever tasted better to me than while camping on this trip. When we had rested a little after eating, we set out again. Generally speaking, the road went through very fertile areas that were largely level and only now and then interspersed with low hills. It was already rather dark when we arrived at our overnight station, the settlement of Mr. Dörst [Abraham Darst]. Since he, like all the other colonists or settlers along the route, maintains a so-called boardinghouse, I spent the night with him. In these houses the standard rate is by meal, whether consisting of breakfast, noon meal, or supper, for ¼ dollar; spending the night costs ⅛ dollar (one bit). Consequently I must advise my countrymen arriving with their families, since they will no doubt be provided with flour, bacon, coffee, and sugar, to choose camping over lodging in these houses. Sleeping in the open with a horse blanket or a mattress cover will not hurt anybody in this warm climate; on the contrary, I, just like the other Germans here, have enjoyed doing this best of all. Since everybody will be carrying his own bedding anyhow, using it will assuredly be more agreeable than what may be encountered in the houses of the Americans; their bedsteads are always very hard, and you sleep with your feet almost as high as your head. This Mr. Darst, who is of German descent, informed me that he used to live in Missouri, where he had known the author of the book about that state [Gottfried Duden], who had settled near him. He referred to him as "doctor," a title Americans use very generously; it is often given to any foreigner not directly

taken to be a workingman or a farmer. Despite my blue travel dust-
er, which would appear to have very little that is doctor-like about
it, even I was on occasion honored with this title. During supper
I got to know a learned Scot by the name of Drummern [Thom-
as Drummond]. As a botanist, he had traveled in all parts of the
United States of North America; but nowhere had he found such
abundance in soil, vegetation, mildness and amenity of climate,
not to mention the easiness of livelihood, as in Texas. Early next
morning Mr. Drummond and I set out even before the wagons and
botanized while slowly walking ahead. Well might Mr. Ernst comment in his letter that he was ashamed of sowing the flower seeds
he had brought along where the carpet of meadowland displays a
continuous show of flowers. I found his phrase entirely confirmed,
even now when the finest and most beautiful species had completed their flowering, March being the showiest time. By agreement
with the teamsters, we once again stopped in a lovely valley. The
trees by the clear creek were displaying a most beautiful vine with
flame-red flowers the size of our tulips, which they also resemble
in fragrance; their shape is trumpet-like. Americans call this flower
cypress vine, though they do not at all belong to this family. The
farther we advanced, the more beautiful the scenery became. Our
further journey was continued in this prescribed manner and got
to be increasingly pleasant for me, as I got to know my mentioned
travel companion more closely. On a Saturday—it was our last stop
before San Felipe—Mr. Drummond, on his excursion, strayed to
the left of the road; I had walked ahead of the wagons by more than
half an hour and suddenly found myself surprised by darkness so
that I could no longer discern the track marks on the road. After
walking still farther ahead, I noticed, at quite some distance to the
right of the road, a fire, recognizing it by the reflection from the
surrounding trees. Since at the same time I encountered several
cows and horses grazing on the road and thought I recognized a
trail here seemingly leading to the fire, I started following it, pre-
suming that I would thus get to our overnight camp, which, according to my figuring, could not be far away. I had hardly pursued my

course for a quarter of an hour when, to my amazement, I found myself in a Spanish colony. Though not conversant with the Spanish language, I approached the people there in a direct and open manner and explained my problem in English. Although the owner of the settlement understood almost nothing of that language, I was nevertheless received in the friendliest manner. Tobacco was fetched right away so that I could fill the pipe he had noticed I carried, and I was served supper. After an hour or so of exchange, largely in pantomime, I was shown to a very clean bed that even had mosquito netting. This usually consists of material similar to gauze and is attached above the bed on posts. I must confess, I was actually a little concerned at first, since I believed I had fallen among Indians; I had my opinion of this strengthened by the fact that one of the Spaniards I encountered here had rather a brownish-yellow appearance. Such is occasionally the case in these parts since, at an earlier time, many Spaniards are said to have interbred with Indians. My concern about possibly being robbed here was, however, not quite without foundation; it was based on the many not exactly flattering accounts Americans had given me about the local Spaniards, and according to which they are said to be strongly inclined toward thievery. I do not consider myself qualified to verify the authenticity of these accounts beyond asserting that at best they apply to the very lowest class of this nation. In instances of passing judgment on entire nations, it is always tempting to draw conclusions based on individuals and apply them in general.

Just after I woke up the next morning, my hospitable host was by my bed to bid me a friendly good morning and to inquire how I had slept. It was a clear and beautiful summer morning, and although the sun was not yet up, I quickly got up, gratefully took leave of my good and friendly host, and started walking in the direction of our appointed overnight camp, which was less than a mile away. When viewed by daylight, this Spanish colonist's settlement was far better than I had expected, since the Spaniards in this country do not often or with much pleasure engage in agricultural pursuits. It included a fine cornfield, quite a neat house built of lumber, and his numerous and good-looking cattle, which gave evidence of rather considerable wealth. I must note that houses of lumber are, to an extent, better here than the conventional log cabins made of entire beams. Only now, by daylight, was I able to enjoy the lovely and attractive area I had come upon by chance. I saw several flocks of game and turkeys with their young, and had to regret that I had left my gun in the wagon, since I had come closer than firing range to the game. Generally speaking, I saw much game on this trip, also later on. This morning stroll delighted me a great deal; the sky was so bright this Sunday morning, a cool refreshing breeze was blowing, and my pleasure was enhanced when I found my lost Scot again right by the encampment at the edge of the woods. He was already botanizing. We now had breakfast together, and both he and our teamsters had a good laugh with me about my little adventure, since it had turned out so well. Since Mr. D. [Drummond] had some plants to arrange here, we agreed to get together again at the establishment of tavern keeper Johns [Jones] in San Felipe. I then continued my journey alone and arrived in the famous capital of Texas at about eleven o'clock. When viewed at a distance from this road, it looks just like a market square out in the open, with its white wooden houses looking like tents and booths. In every respect, the appearance of San Felipe is much more pleasant than that of Brazoria. The town is situated on the prairie, which has a very picturesque aspect here, alternating as it does with great variety between hills, valleys, and bushy areas. On one side the site has the Brazos River rolling past; it being quite low just then, the banks were rather steep. The river is quite yellow in color, appearing almost darker still than below at Brazoria. At Mr. Jones' tavern I found a letter from Schwarting, my former travel companion; he was staying with a German farmer (settler), Mr. [Charles] Fordtran, on Mill Creek and invited me to join him, but I had very good reasons to stick to my plan and go to Mr. Ernst's instead. Even now I have every good cause to be satisfied with my choice, with the fine Ernst family endeavoring right up to this very moment to make life pleasant for me. I learned from tavern keeper Jones, with whom I was staying, that there was a certain Mr. [James] Miles in San Felipe who would be passing by the Ernst settlement the following day, Monday, on his return trip; Jones was obliging enough to take me to the man's lodging. It was agreed that I would go there right after breakfast the following morning so we could set out and travel together. Next day I did not for a moment tarry in following my instructions, since I had a burning desire finally to reach the destination of my long journey. However, since Mr. Miles, as he stated, still had this and that to take care of and, as it seemed to me, was not in a particularly great hurry, I had him give me directions and started out alone. However, this haste cost me dearly and really brought home the truth of the old adage of making haste slowly. What happened was that I had the unenviable pleasure of walking twenty-four miles entirely for nothing, and this indeed on a very hot day and with my knapsack packed. I had left my belongings at the trading house of Perry and Somervell and taken only items needed for the time being, for a change, etc. However, strictly speaking, I could console myself that I had been innocent about this unfortunate trip, for when I asked Mr. Miles if I should not just keep walking straight ahead, he confirmed; so I really could not but follow directions. Most likely he did not understand me correctly, since I should have turned right at the very beginning. On this trip I turned around quite often while walking to see if my expected travel companion was not approaching, but always in vain. It may have been around two o'clock in the afternoon when I finally came to a wide creek, which had dried up enough for me to cross with my shoes on, and which had a sandy bed, quite white. I had still not seen any sign of a settlement anywhere where I could have inquired about directions, and was thus all the more surprised to find some of the teamsters I knew from the trip to San Felipe camped by the water. Upon my asking if I was going the right way, I heard to my considerable dismay that I was heading straight for the Colorado River. From where I was right then, I had already covered twelve miles. When I inquired more closely of the good and honest teamsters, who truly appeared to sympathize with my misfortune, I learned that there was no other way to remedy the situation than to turn around, return to San Felipe, and resume my travel the following Tuesday morning. With my decision made directly, it was carried into action just as promptly, and even if there had been a shorter route to my destination there was still cause to prefer returning. I quickened my pace and was fortunate enough to return to San Felipe around ten o'clock in the evening. The following morning, I hurried straightaway to storekeeper [Heinrich] Klönne [Henry Klonne], a German, to get his help in finding a guide. I had hardly entered into conversation with him when—to my great surprise and delight—my former travel companion, Mr. Scherrer, entered the store and reported to me that he was ready with a wagon and a riding horse. A better opportunity could certainly not be found. It was a hot day, and since the owner of the wagon, Mr. Ernst's neighbor, did not want to leave until about evening, this quite agreed with me. Since Mr. Scherrer's horse was running about on the prairie, our joint search for it gave me an opportunity at the same time to explore the immediate vicinity of San Felipe. It was during this excursion that we came upon Colonel Austin's house, where the land office is located; we entered to register our names for the distribution of land. However, it is closed at the moment since the colonel is away on travel. As we learned here, a few leagues are still available in Austin's Colony, these being from individuals who did not take possession and thus have lapsed. The colonel's house is in an interesting location and is the most beautiful one I had so far seen in Texas. Laid out in an attractive valley, before it there is a high gently rising elevation, covered in small sections with natural vegetation of oaks, mulberries, sycamores, etc., as if human hand had turned it into an English garden. In the background a creek clear as crystal runs in a deep bed through natural shrubbery and over rocks; at high water levels, it goes out of its banks and floods the immediate vicinity. However, one thing I regretted the house not having was a beautiful garden. It seems, generally speaking, that Americans only cherish whatever produces money and derive but little pleasure, even when they are wealthy,

Figure 8. A crossing on the San Bernard River. "It may have been around two
o'clock in the afternoon when I finally came to a wide creek, which had
dried up enough for me to cross with my shoes on, and which
had a sandy bed, quite white." Photo by Geir Bentzen.

from such planned amenable installations that combine usefulness
and beauty, and for which nature herself provides such vigorous
encouragement.

In San Felipe there is a billiards room, as well as several taverns,
of which I particularly want to recommend to my countrymen the
establishment of Mr. Jones, since it provides the most courteous
service.

At four o'clock in the afternoon we finally started on our journey, which only continued while we were able to see comfortably.
We stopped by a spring in a lovely valley, which displayed itself
all the more strikingly the following morning by the full daylight
of the bright morning sun. This particular day I felt uncommonly
happy. My travel companions were also in a good mood, and our
black coffee with dry bread tasted magnificent as we were camped

around the fire. We soon resumed our travel. The scenery became increasingly less tame and more beautiful, though there was no decline whatever in fertility; the highest elevations, whether they were wooded or not, indicated to us the most productive soil. Mr. Scherrer and I took turns riding, which, after my earlier unfortunate express race, was a great relief. I might well have good reason to feel happy on this day; it was the day on which I was to reach the destination of my journey. My journey of several thousand miles had now been completed safely and without accidents of any consequence; indeed, I had cause to thank the Almighty silently in my heart for this act of grace. It was six o'clock in the evening when I arrived at the settlement of the beloved Ernst family, and the hospitable and affectionate reception of these kind people could only enhance my cheerfulness even more. I spent a very delightful evening, which I shall always remember with pleasure. The closer I got to the Ernst settlement, the more the ideal I had formed from his letter was confirmed. Here I found once again the charming fields of the eastern Holstein of my fatherland, and was often most pleasantly surprised by deceptive similarities in scenery. Mr. Ernst's house is located in an attractive valley. In the foreground there is a hill of considerable elevation with a few picturesque wooded areas. To the left of the elevation are gray rocks covered with [undisturbed] native shrubbery, under which several springs with the clearest water are gushing forth, one of them diverted to a lower level to irrigate the small garden, another for the same purpose to the area cultivated for farming. In the distance the cornfields border on a wooded area through which Mill Creek flows; it is named for a mill established on it about twenty miles from here. The high hill already mentioned provides a magnificent view of the natural romantic scenery, which nevertheless cannot be referred to as wilderness, there being nowhere a single plant of heather in sight. There is only green expanse, hills and valleys covered with individual stands of trees, high woodlands, brush, the most beautiful flowers, shining herds of cattle, and also flocks of deer. Against the horizon are hills and woodlands of still higher elevation, and an immense distance away there extends, through the deep valley of Mill Creek, a long band of primeval forest. Though the day after my arrival in this little Elysium had been intended for rest, in the company of Mr. Scherrer I climbed the hills nearest by, roamed about in the woods, and there I had an invigorating bath in Mill Creek, which I enjoyed very much, having had for several years to forgo such pleasures because of lack of a suitable bathing site. The following day I visited my Oldenburg countryman, Mr. Schwarting; on the way over I got acquainted with another Oldenburg family, that of Dr. [Johann Diedrich Georg] Varrelmann. He was the first one to leave for Texas in response to the Ernst letter. He has taken over a quarter league from Mr. Fordtran and already established himself. Because of heavy rain, I had to stay at Mr. Schwarting's for two days; Mr. Fordtran gave me a very fine reception here. He is very clever at mechanical work; he had thus done repair work on a hunting gun that would have done honor to the finest locksmith. The area around this colony is also very interesting; the dwelling-house is situated up high, and there are already several small houses clustered around, and my only regret is that there is no garden. Nor is the dwelling-house as presentable as Mr. Ernst's, though it is much more substantial. As he states in his letter, Mr. Ernst has built his little house in the style of his garden house in Oldenburg. It is hexagonal, and with its modest thatched roof and white color quite presentable.

At the moment that I am writing this, after having been here for so long in order to slowly check everything and see for myself, I can assure all of my German countrymen that Mr. Ernst's letter, reproduced in the introduction, was completely confirmed in all particulars. Indeed, Texas is a country where conditions are made as easy for the immigrant who wants to pursue agriculture as they are anywhere else in the world, certainly to this extent—it is a land that puts riches in his lap, that can bring happiness to thousands and to their descendants—it is a country just waiting for people so that our European industry can raise and elevate it to the most blessed country in all the known world, and certainly the central

Figure 9. Field picture: "The high hill already mentioned provides a magnificent view of the natural romantic scenery [. . .]." Present-day view of the valley of the Ernst settlement from the hill above.
Photo by Geir Bentzen.

government could have only this purpose in mind when it, as my readers will learn in more detail below, accorded immigrant Europeans such great opportunities.

Many will hardly believe how fast, for example, the growth of all plants is here, until they see it with their own eyes. Thus I found at my arrival several chinaberry trees planted in front of the house, which, in the span of 1½ months, produced new growth of five feet. There are many plants here that can be harvested three times.

All immigrants who set out to come here, and who might not immediately have an opportunity to have a suitable league assigned, can still advance themselves. Any American or German farmer will welcome them to farm on his land for the time being. Nobody is particular about it; on the contrary, they find it desirable to turn over to immigrants as much land as they can manage to put into cultivation, and this without figuring on rent or lease money in return. Since the immigrant should then give his highest priority to cattle, which will find their own feed in abundance everywhere on the extensive landholdings, he will then be completely set up to take possession of his own league. Even people of limited means, if they perceive in themselves the desire and strength to work, can easily get ahead in this manner. Even when, at some time in the future, all land laid out will have been assigned, many people can still be helped out in this manner. Even though most land in this old colony has found owners already, it can still be purchased from them for ¼ dollar per acre and probably even less, whereas in the United States the price, though lowered, still amounts to 1¼ dollar per acre, and farm products there are hardly half of what they are here. These are certainly opportunities that thousands in Europe would reach out for.

FURTHER OBSERVATIONS
CONCERNING TEXAS.

Report on the Most Essential Parts of the
Colonization Law and the Constitutional Acts.

AS NOTED ABOVE, most of the land laid out in this Austin colony is already occupied. However, to the west it borders on the new, or upper, colony; this has a still higher elevation, has just as fertile soil as the former, and on average even exceeds it in lofty, romantic scenery. Since the colony is located on the Brazos and, moreover, there is no dearth of water transport there, the marketing of products is ensured. As to the clearest and finest drinking water, as well as woodlands, there is no shortage anywhere. A great deal of cedar is found here, and also pine; the former is rather rare in Austin's Colony, though it is highly prized, while the latter is found in only a few areas. As to game, the new colony has a similar abundance. How much would beautiful Texas be improved by further immigration is entirely beyond calculation, but I must still note on this occasion that those Germans who are resolved to this end must not tarry too long with their ocean crossing, since the pressure of Americans from the United States is very great and consequently the best land is easily sold out. As has just been mentioned, nobody here is lacking when it comes to elementary needs. I, too, have settled at Mr. Ernst's for the time being, for which purpose I have already purchased the necessary cattle. It remains to be seen whether I shall take land here or in the upper colony, after the land office resumes its functions later this fall.

Just as the fine soil, romantic scenery, etc., will appeal to my countrymen, so will they have cause to be pleased with the local climate as well. I will be glad to admit that even after reading the Ernst letter I had imagined the heat to be more considerable than I have found to be the case. Even though it does, indeed, rise to higher levels on average than in Germany, the air in turn is all the lighter, particularly in these hilly, more elevated regions; it never becomes as oppressive and exhausting as during our dog days, and there is no lack of cooling breezes, something we often miss so much in Germany. As was mentioned, on a very hot day, with my knapsack packed, I went on a hike of twenty-four miles here and can assure my readers that I was less strained by heat doing this than on similar trips during the heat of summer in Germany. Here you can expose yourself more boldly to any kind of draft or chance of catching cold than we are used to, without suffering from coughing, sniffles, etc. The air is so pure here that during the fine summer evenings, the stars have a splendor comparable to what we know from the most biting freezing weather. Along with Mr. Ernst and two other Germans staying here, I have already been sleeping out in the open under the trees by the house for more than two months, and I can honestly say that I have never enjoyed finer sleep.

In addition to the Germans living here—amounting to twelve men or heads of families, not counting women and children—I have already visited several American families in the vicinity, among them highly respectable individuals worthy of esteem. Many of them have been in all twenty-six provinces of the free states of North America; all of these colonists also confirm what was said by Mr. Drummond about Texas, that this country by far exceeds those states in every respect.

The first colonization law stipulated that only Europeans and no Americans were to be admitted for settlement in this country, since the concerns of the New Mexicans [the citizens of the Mexican republic] toward the neighboring country still seemed to be entertained. Despite the generous grant on the part of the new government of an enormous quantity of land for each family—according to the contract of the *empresarios*—as well as public guarantee of security of person and property, civil liberties, and citizenship, and tax exemption for several years—despite all of this, as well as the fine climate of the country being an attractive enticement for anybody who was inclined or compelled to look for a new home—even so, the very nation itself and its intent was too unknown to most individuals in other countries for Mexico to have been able to achieve its purpose quickly. And even assuming that individual European immigrants were better informed, still the political disturbances and instability of the mother country of Mexico might have prompted these people to prefer the free states of North America.

For a number of years now the new settlers had been sitting in deep solitude on their recently established property, often several days distant from their closest neighbors, almost cut off from association with the civilized world, though in possession of raw natural resources. But because of such isolation, these resources could only be used to satisfy basic needs and in most instances people had only their own ingenuity to depend on; the more refined pleasures of life, to which civilized man is accustomed, were largely out of the question. Only the hope of a better future, brought about by a larger population to come, allowed them to patiently endure. The arguments of the authorized *empresario* finally persuaded the government to stop closing the door on his countrymen, the Americans. The quota of families stipulated in the first contract was quickly filled and major and minor conditions thus satisfied. For every one hundred families introduced, the *empresario* received as his own property an accorded quantity of land. Now new contracts were made, all of which were satisfied in due course.

To acquaint my readers more closely with the desire of the Mexican government and the spirit of the laws designed to apply to the population plan for Texas, it might not be unwarranted to make mention in the following of some of these articles of law.

In the first article of the [national] colonization law d.d. [*de dato*]

August 18, 1824, the Mexican nation offers foreigners who wish to settle in its territory security of person and property, provided they subject themselves to the laws of the country. In Article 7 the Congress relinquishes its own authority to prohibit the admittance of any foreigner, provided considerations involving another nation do not render it necessary. Article 14 guarantees the contract of the *empresario* with the introduced colonists, and Article 15 refuses anyone acquisition of land obtained under that law who does not reside within the boundaries of the republic (a well-advised measure for promoting the purpose of the law and for the benefit of its citizens). Another national law of April 6, 1830, was published with reference to some articles of colonization for the territory of the republic. It prohibits admitting foreigners from the northern boundary without warrant of their good intention, demands strict observance of the colonization law on the part of the states, and prohibits the importation of slaves. It prohibits citizens of foreign areas bordering on American territory from settling in those parts of the republic bordering their previous residence, and it revokes the conditions which are contrary to that article. It opens coastal trade for four years to foreign ships for the transport of the colony's products to Matamoros, Tampico, and Vera Cruz—and exempts from duty for two years the importation of cut lumber and every kind of food item to the ports of Galveston and Matagorda. The permanent principles of the colonization law of 1824, some of which have been cited, have been kept completely in force by the legislative authority of Coahuila and Texas, and in the state law of March 24, 1825, settlers and contractors are granted such concessions as could promise them the greatest measure of success in populating the territory of the state. The fact that this aim has been attained so slowly is due to unfamiliarity with the law's design. The introductory part of this law confirms the government's intentions in language that demands the greatest confidence; even the self-interest of the state vouches for its good intentions, with both being sanctioned by the honor of the Castillian nation, which is expressed in these words, "The Constitutional Congress of the free, independent, and sovereign state of Coahuila and Texas, desiring by every possible means to increase the population of its territory, to promote the cultivation of its fertile land, the raising and increase of livestock, advancement of the arts and of commerce, and being governed by the constitutional acts, the federal constitution, and the basis established by national Decree No. 72 of the General Congress, has thought it proper to make public the following law of colonization: Art. 1. All foreigners, who by virtue of the general law of August 18, 1824, which guaranteed security of person and of property within the territory of the Mexican nation, desire to move as inhabitants to the State of Coahuila and Texas, are freely invited to do so." The second article assures those who intend to move here that rather than facing interference (this probably had reference to the late Spanish administration), they will be entirely free to pursue any branch of industry. The third and fourth articles permit any foreign settler to take up residence by declaring this intention to the local authority, and he is at liberty to choose any vacant land for his residence. Articles 8 and 9 authorize contracting for purposes of colonization and repeat the guarantee of the national government with regard to the contracts of *empresarios* with families introduced at their expense. Article 22 establishes that within six years of settlement, three dollars and fifty cents will be paid as acknowledgment for each *labor* of irrigated land, and Articles 38 and 39 order that the government issue titles to the colonists, who, as stipulated by the contractors, determine the commissioner's and the surveyor's fees together with the parties in question. Other than these expenditures and those for stamps and titles, nothing in the form of taxes and contributions is required by law of the new colonist, except for what is undertaken jointly by everybody and what families of legal standing willingly impose on themselves to maintain community institutions such as ferries, roads, schools, etc. The 32nd Article contains the encouraging stipulation, "During the first ten years—calculated from the day of occupancy—the settlement shall be free of all taxes and contributions of whatever designation, with the exception of those which imperative circumstances might demand in case of enemy invasion or its prevention. All products of agriculture and industry of the new settlers shall be free of any tax or excise duty (*Alcabala*) throughout every part of the state, except for the tax on mines. After the termination of this time, the new settler shall be on the same footing with the other inhabitants." In addition to this ten-year tax exemption, there is further liberality in the laws, even concerning imported items for personal use; the colonist is also granted the privilege of a free citizen to vote in municipal elections and even to be elected himself. Article 46 decrees that the law be made known in all localities in the state and be reported to the legislative powers of other states, as well as to the General Congress so that it may circulate among foreign nations through ambassadors. Before the world, the government has most solemnly promised to fulfill the obligations to which it has bound itself by law. In addition to the provisions contained in the law, the instructions of the land commissioner are established under the administration of the legislature: that he must scrupulously examine the contract between the *empresario* and the government and the colonization laws, as well as the morality of the new colonist. The legislature determines the manner in which settlers obtain their titles as follows, "The commissioner shall issue in the name of the state the titles for land, in conformity with the law, and then put the colonist in possession of his new land, with all legal formalities after previous announcement to adjoining property owners, should there be any." His other obligations are to lay out towns and communities according to baselines running north to south and east to west, to establish ferries and roads, and to preside over local elections, etc. Since with this the major colonization laws and instructions have now been touched upon with regard to their more interesting substance, it would be unnecessary to make mention of further decrees, since these would be of less interest to my good readers. It might be of greater interest to them to get acquainted in the following with the form and authority of the Mexican government. As already mentioned by Mr. Ernst in the letter referred to several times, the legal constitution of the Mexican republic is modeled on that of North America; but on the presupposition that a majority of readers might not be acquainted with the latter, a closer examination might not be considered unnecessary.

The Mexican republic consists of eighteen [nineteen] states and five [four] territories, the latter under the direct administration of the central government, whereas the former, the states, have their separate legislatures, all of them under one general, or federal, government. The form of government is republican and representative. It consists of an executive authority that answers to the president, who is elected for four years and is not eligible again until after the course of another four years; of an independent judiciary, and a legislative body of two departments. The General Congress is empowered as follows: to preserve national independence; to be concerned with national security and to maintain foreign relations; to uphold the federal union of the states and to maintain public law and order within the country; to preserve the independence of the states among themselves and to support their relative equality as to duties and rights; chiefly, it has the authority to guide and maintain all federal relations. The powers of the state government of Coahuila and Texas are vested in a governor, a legislature, and a judiciary, just like those of the United States of North America, based on the following prescribed decrees, among others: "Everybody who inhabits the territory of the state shall enjoy the irrevocable rights of liberty, security of property, and equality; and it is a public duty to preserve and protect these universal rights of the human race by wise and equitable laws. It is also an obligation for the state to protect all of its inhabitants in the rights which they possess, of writing, printing, and freely publishing their thoughts and political opinions, without the necessity of examination, review, or censorship, previous to their publications. In this country nobody shall be born a slave, nor shall the introduction of slaves be permitted under any pretext. Foreigners who truly and legally settle in the state are citizens, without regard to their country of birth." In the constitution, the provision is made that "Every citizen can terminate his controversies by arbitration, whatever the status of the case, by means of arbitrators or in any extrajudicial manner; all agreements of decision are to be considered sacred. In the majority of cases no court warrants can be issued until a friendly conciliation has been attempted in the manner prescribed by law." Public education is established on the following basis: "In all towns of the state, a suitable number of schools shall be established, in which reading, writing, arithmetic, and the catechism of the Christian religion are taught, as well as a brief and simple explanation of the constitution and of the republic, of the rights and duties of man in society, and everything conducive to the useful and agreeable education of the young. The method of teaching shall be uniform throughout the state. In places where it is considered necessary, special institutions shall be established which are suitable for the purpose of providing preparation for public education."

It could not fail that a country so rich in opportunities as Texas, with a constitution so similar to that of the North American union, would soon become well known and enticing to the Americans, who are so enterprising and venturesome. So they did not tarry in accepting the concessions that were granted to them as immigrants, and it is believed that in a span of six years close to six thousand people emigrated from there to the newly established colony. The advantages that the colonization law offered the *empresarios* for every one hundred families introduced now also prompted several of them to make contracts directly with the government. However, on the whole, they may not have been as successful in their endeavors as Colonel Austin, for which their own not altogether proper conduct was probably to blame. Several of Austin's grants[5] were already populated; they already included the two major rivers, the Brazos and the Colorado, and extended all the way to the coast, uniting within themselves the most beautiful and favorable areas. Even though some sites were laid out strictly for Europeans, the authorities were now less stern toward the Americans and generally made less of a fuss with other nations, keeping in mind their main purpose, which was to populate the colonies; moreover, there was no shortage of land whatsoever in Texas, which obviated the practice of continually earmarking part of it for Europeans. In order to familiarize the gentle reader and prospective immigrant in more detail with the land distributions and the quantities that are available for agriculture, as well as with the aforementioned grants, I shall briefly call attention to some articles of the [national] colonization law of March 24, 1825: "Article 11. A square of land, which on each side has one league[6] or five thousand *varas*, shall be called a *sitio*. This shall constitute the unit for counting such as: one, two, or several *sitios*, as it shall constitute as well the unit for counting: one, two, or several *labores*. A million *varas*, or one thousand *varas* on each side, shall constitute a *labor*. Article 12. Taking the above unit as a basis and observing the distinction between pasture or grassland and what is suitable for farming and easy to irrigate, this law grants to the contractor, for the settlement of every one hundred families that he introduces and establishes in the state, five *sitios* of grassland and five *labores*, of which half is without irrigation. But they can only receive this premium for eight hundred families, even though a larger number may be introduced, and no fraction, whatever it may be, of less than a hundred shall entitle them to any premium, not even proportionally. Article 13. If a contractor, as a result of the number of families introduced, in conformity with the last article, should acquire more than eleven leagues of land, it shall nevertheless be granted, but the excess must be subject to being parceled out within twelve years, and if this is not done, the proper authority shall carry it out by selling the excess land at a public sale and delivering the proceeds to the owner, after the deduction of costs. Article 14. To each family included in a contract, whose only occupation is cultivation of land, shall be given a *labor* of land. If, however, the family is occupied with stock raising, grassland shall be added so as to constitute a *sitio*; and if its only occupation is the raising of stock, then only a surface area of twenty-four [twenty-five] million bars [*varas*]. Article 15. Unmarried men shall receive the same quantity when they enter into marriage. Foreigners who marry native Mexican women shall receive one-fourth more. Those who are entirely single or do not constitute part of a family, neither foreign or native, shall content themselves with the fourth part of the above, which is all that can be granted them before they marry. Article 16. Families or unmarried men who immigrate entirely of their own accord, and who wish to unite for the establishment of a new town, are free to do so at all times, and the same quantity of land shall be given to them as was mentioned in the last two articles. But if they unite for this purpose within the first six years of their settlement, then families shall be given one additional *labor* and unmarried men instead of a fourth (as stated in Article 15), shall have a third of a *sitio*. Article 17. It is within the purview of the government to increase the quantity of land indicated in the 14th, 15th, and 16th Articles in proportion to the industry of any given family and its activity, in keeping with the information supplied by the local authorities and commissioners, as said government observes the provisions of the 12th Article of the decree of the General Congress as it applies to this subject. Article 18. Families that immigrate according to the 16th Article shall immediately present themselves before the authorities near the place that they have chosen for their residence; upon finding them complying with the requirements of the law, the authorities will admit them and put them into possession of their respective lands and immediately notify the government, which directly or through a commissioned person will issue a title to this effect. Article 22. The new settler shall, as an acknowledgment, pay for each *sitio* of grassland thirty dollars, for each *labor* without good irrigation two-and-one-half dollars, and so on in proportion to the quantity and quality of the land distributed. But said payments do not have to be made for six years and can be made by thirds, so that the first third is to be paid after four years, the second after five, and the remainder after six years, under penalty of loss of the land in case of failure to pay. Exempt from this payment are contractors and military persons, mentioned in the 10th Article, the former with regard to landholdings given them as a premium, and the latter in accord with properties received with their commissions. Article 24.

The government will sell to Mexicans and only to them such land as they wish to buy, while considering that the same party not be given more than eleven leagues, and on the condition that the purchaser must cultivate the land to which he has title within six years, under penalty of loss of the land. Subject to the aforementioned conditions, the price of each *sitio* shall amount to one hundred dollars, if it is land for agriculture without easy irrigation, and two hundred and fifty dollars, if it can be irrigated. Article 26. The new settler who within six years of the date of his taking possession has not cultivated the land granted him or has it in use in proportion to its quality, shall be considered as having relinquished it, and the pertinent authority shall revoke the title and take possession.[7] Article 29. Land obtained under this law cannot by any title, of whatever kind, be forfeited in seizure or attachment (Manus Muertos [Manos muertas]). Article 30. The new settler who is contemplating establishing himself in a foreign region is free to do so with all his property. But after he has left the state, he shall no longer keep his land; if he has not sold it already, or if the sale is not in agreement with Article 27, it shall become entirely vacant."

Certainly, no one will fail to notice that all of these laws express a very benevolent spirit, especially as far as Europeans are concerned, and these land gifts, as the distributions might well be called, leave nothing to be desired by the immigrant; they are not known to be exceeded on any continent. Only Brazil might be an exception to this; it cannot be denied that at one time the offers there were even more enticing. However, at the moment, because of the disturbances that have broken out there, less is known about the status of colonization there, and it may easily have come to a complete standstill. And even assuming that such is not the case, still the moral constraint and clericalism prevailing there would be quite an impediment for new colonists, something which is not to be feared at all in the free Mexican republic, though at its very establishment a law did exist that only the Roman Catholic religion was to be considered the religion of the country—because of resulting dissatisfaction concerning this subject, it was erased, and consequently everybody now enjoys full freedom of religion. Great are the opportunities that Texas offers to commerce, not merely through the mother country of Mexico, but also by way of the great neighboring country and, as a result of its own productivity, soon, one must hope, with Europe as well. North America, inhabited by one of the greatest and most enlightened nations—with territory bordering Texas on two sides and its population quickly increasing in this direction—in which thousands long ago have found a sanctuary and a government recognizing the true and just rights of humanity, dwelled in by a peace-loving people, equally alien to any wild desire to conquer and to misguiding despots, partial also to a rational rather than a fraudulent concept of liberty, with a wise and prudent government, at the head of which is one of the greatest men of his people, a nation which only draws its sword when its noblest possession, its freedom, is endangered—having such a country for a neighbor is certainly to be considered a great blessing; and it opens the pleasant prospect of enduring, neighborly peace, the very opposite of what the history of the Old World teaches in too many instances. If that spirit is not yet prevalent to such a degree in this new country, it must be kept in mind how new it still is, that it arose from the ashes of a government that was not exactly favorable, and that first the Spanish people in Mexico must learn to become fond of the salutary condition it has been placed in by virtue of its constitutional acts.

Earlier in these pages thought was given to the new, or upper, colony; it is laid out for eight hundred families, indeed specifically for European ones, a reservation expressly made by the government with the comment that no Americans be granted admittance to this colony. Nevertheless, the way things are now, whoever happens to arrive enters, regardless of what country he may belong to. At the moment, it is not quite clear who the proper contractor is; however, this uncertain status will soon change and no longer be an obstruction to the immigrant. The new colony also presents the impressive spectacle of a waterfall, which the Brazos forms here. It may be located about two hundred miles in a straight line from its mouth; though it may not suffer comparison with the Niagara between lakes Ontario and Erie in the state of New York, it still might be the most significant one after the waterfall at Schaffhausen. To acquaint the reader better with the grants laid out in Texas, here follows a list of them:

Austin's grant	1,100 families
A second Austin do.	100 \²
The disputed grant[8]	800 \²
Telisola's [Filisola's][9] do.	600 \²
Barnett's [Burnet's] do.	300 \²
Chilin's [Vehlein's] do.	300 \²
Cameron's do.	200 \²
Cameron's second grant	100 \²
Mullen & Gloin's [McMullen and McGloin's]	200 \²
Martín de León	150 \²

Three additional ones without definite number listed as:

Zavalle's [Zavala's] grant.
Devid's [DeWitt's] do.
Pover's [Power's] do.

The grants with definite numbers, combined, come to 3,850 families
The indefinite ones, judging by their sizes, approximately about 500 \²
The premium accorded *empresarios* might be assumed to be 50 \²

Thus, not more than 4,400 families; if each one occupied a *sitio*, only 39,000 miles would be distributed.

Texas extends four hundred miles along the coast and holds the ports of Galveston and Matagorda—the former is the better and is considered the most excellent one between Pensacola, Florida, and Vera Cruz in Mexico; it is located directly on the Gulf and has free access to all coastal locations of its confederated states, such as Tampico, Matagorda, Alvordo [Alvarado], Vera Cruz, and the Bay of Campeche; to the left, the United States; right in front of it in the ocean, only a few days' voyage away, the rich island of Cuba; farther to the right, the other West Indian islands. It is to be considered the center of all America. The path of the Gulf Stream passes by and dispatches the ships on their courses to the eastern and the Atlantic Ocean. The state of Texas has so far been associated with Coahuila, and the governor had his seat in the latter province, in Santilla [Saltillo]. Petition has already been made for Texas to constitute a separate state, which, from what one hears, is reported to have been granted. Coahuila only borders on Texas by a narrow strip and, in view of its location, has only little association with it. The inhabitants of the former lay little claim to culture; they are, except for the coastal sites, Mexicans of the old school, and from all reports there is not much to be said in their praise, unless it be—that they devote themselves to horse stealing.

In Germany, especially in Bremen, there was much commotion about disturbances having erupted in Mexico; it was even alleged that in Texas there was no safety of person or property whatever. This latter statement I must refute altogether; nothing is known here of instances of theft, and how little one has to be fearful of such is proved by the fact that on no house can a lock be found. Stealing will not easily occur to anybody here, since making a livelihood here is so easy. Incidentally, as to the disturbances that erupted, there is not much substance to those, either. Between Brazoria and the mouth of the Brazos there is an old mud wall, which some call a fortress and others refer to as the "Chicken House." This old haunt was occupied by some Mexican soldiers. The purpose of this garrison might not have been to prevent a possible invasion on the part of the Americans; it seems more likely that the government had detached this military unit to protect the levy of entrance fees, or to provide help to the new colonists against possible Indian incursions. However, in a manner quite contrary to these beneficial purposes, the garrison permitted itself to engage in many acts of violence against the inhabitants. When the Mexican garrison made the situation too insufferable in the summer of 1832, a regular desire to fight arose in the American colonists; being quite aware of their shooting skill, they did not wait, but took over the various garrisoned locations, one after the other, with only about a hundred men. The number of troops in Nacogdoches was indicated at nine hundred men. The Americans carried their fortifications around with them; these consisted of thick boards with a base for the riflemen to stand on. The shooting skill of almost all American colonists is very great; wherever they saw as much as a Spanish head above the barricades, it would be the end of that soldier. However, several Americans were also wounded, for which their wooden fortifications were responsible; they were shot through, and very often the rifleman standing behind them was wounded by the rebounding splinters. As the oppressed, when their freedom is threatened, are always strong against their tormentors, so it also happened here. Once during this fight, six riflemen took twenty fully armed dragoons prisoner, along with their horses, and had them lay down their arms. In such small skirmishes, it was apparent at least that the spirit of the great Washington was not extinguished in them. General [Antonio López de] Santa Anna, who had received a very distorted rumor of this unequal fight, dispatched a colonel [José Antonio Mexía] with sufficient force to the location, to investigate the circumstances more closely. When the officers of this expedition had landed, and when the purpose of their mission became known, they were received in the friendliest manner by the citizens; they came to an understanding about the incident and concluded the whole business with a ball. Now those who had started the problems were taken to Mexico, to be held accountable, and the garrison that had aroused the distrust was removed for the time being. Only for a short time at first did these misdeeds put a stop to the desire to immigrate, and the humane views of the government were quickly apparent; it is assumed that with the quickly resumed immigrations, the population has now risen to twenty thousand inhabitants. With regard to the previously mentioned article about a projected plan for Texas to be an independent state, it must be mentioned in retrospect that the colonists convened at a meeting, after which it was unanimously agreed to submit a petition, in which the great distance from the seat of government and all plausible reasons were combined and the formation of a separate state requested. A paper published in Brazoria supposedly reports the request has been granted, based on reliable information. This circumstance and change of status, as soon as it is realized, can only be of great advantage to Texas. Apart from the fact that it thus achieves more weight among the other states, it can accordingly make more demands to have its interests more reliably secured, and the citizens will save many long and expensive road and travel expenses.

Peopling Texas could best be done by Americans, and certainly it was a wise decision on the part of the Mexican Congress to no longer put up barriers against emigration from that country. Probably no people would be better suited as founders of a new country, still to be developed, than the Americans. For the most part, they themselves were born in a country that more resembled a desert than the charming Texas meadows; in early youth they were trained to a hardy way of life, acquainted with all the requirements of the primary cultivation of a country, the forests of which had never been touched by an axe nor its sod by a plow. Where a European, accustomed to a softer way of life, might complain about deprivations, the American was content and cheerful, willing to be satisfied with the yields of his herds, his field, his hunting. He stands patient and brave in the face of all difficulties and dangers; nothing will mislead him, and with or without a compass he travels through wilderness untrod by human foot, merely following his sense of direction, gifted with a sort of instinct similar to that of the Indian.

It is to be hoped that it will be of some interest to the reader to find a few more articles from the national law of April 6, 1830, since they do throw more light on the intention of the General Congress with regard to population and cultivation of this country. Among other regulations, it states as follows:

Article 1.[10] The importation of any kind of cotton goods prohibited in the law of May 22 shall be permitted until January 1, 1831, in all ports of the republic, and in those that are located on the south sea, until June 1, 1831. Article 2. The importation duties on the introduction of such goods shall be used to preserve the indivisibility of the Mexican territory; for the formation of a reserve fund to be used in the event of a Spanish invasion, and for the stimulation of the national industry. Article 7. Mexican families who of their own free will desire to become colonists, shall be given free transportation, maintained during the first year, and be given a quantity of land as well as farm implements. Article 10. With regard to the colonies already established, no change shall be made concerning the slaves that are actually in these colonies. But both the general government as well as that of the individual states shall practice the strictest observance of the colonization law and prevent further importation of slaves. Article 12. For and during a period of four years, coastal trade shall be free for foreign ships for the transportation of colonial products to the seaports of Matamoros, Tampico, and Vera Cruz. Article 14. The government is empowered and authorized to spend the sum of five hundred thousand dollars for the construction of fortresses and public buildings on the frontiers, for the removal of convicts and Mexican families to the new colonies, for their maintenance with residence and farm implements, for the removal of troops, for premiums for agriculture if colonists might distinguish themselves, and for the promotion of the chief purposes of the foregoing articles. Article 15. For the purpose of prompt procurement of half of the sum mentioned, the government is authorized to negotiate a loan to be paid from the customs duties on rough cotton goods at the rate of 3 percent, according to the stipulation established by the *aroncel*.[11] Article 16. One-twentieth of the above-mentioned import duty shall be used for the encouragement of cotton manufacturers, for the procurement of machines and looms, to advance small sums to assist with their establishment, and by any other means that the government might deem useful where these branches of industry are practiced. The distribution shall be at the disposal of the minister of foreign affairs and be directed toward the above-indicated matters in question. Article 17. Similarly, of the amount of the aforementioned import duty, one hundred thousand dollars shall be reserved for the establishment of a fund, which is to be deposited in the treasury, under the strictest responsibility that it not be seized, except if a Spanish attack were to occur.

It is clear how far the Mexican Congress has extended its protection to its native-born population through provisions appropriate to the needs of the times. The measures taken here were not considered necessary in the United States, where admittedly there was less need of them, since European immigrants had poured in throughout its history; close to one hundred thousand persons are said to have immigrated to the United States in recent years. Most of the people came from the oppressed country of Ireland; however, there were also many Germans among them. Last fall in Bremen I was assured that from that location alone thirty thousand people, especially from Hesse and other areas of the upper Weser River, had immigrated to America. In May of this year an English newspaper asserted that twenty thousand had taken ship from Hamburg for the United States.

I cannot refrain from calling my reader's attention to a few additional items, which I hope will not be entirely gratuitous.

If in Germany young, sturdy people can be found who know how to work and have the seventy to eighty Reichsthaler required to get here, then in a few years, if fortune will favor them just a little, they will be established. For if they work for an American and have a good opportunity to learn English, they can earn ten dollars a month for average work; maids doing quite conventional work get five dollars, and if they qualify as cooks and know how to iron and do laundry, they earn ten to fifteen dollars. If young men do not have the opportunity or the desire to work for others—although in such a relationship they are treated entirely as gentlemen and are even given the title of Mister and put virtually on an equal footing with the family, sharing meals, etc.—even so, as workingmen they can also earn their dollar a day by boarding somewhere where they can live rather cheaply, often for a dollar per week. Should they not wish to take this latter approach, they can always put up a house on some farmer's land, which will cost them little or nothing; often they will have an opportunity here to have the use of some cows for the time being, and also, on request, as much land as they need will be turned over to them.

Should you get married, you can have a league of land assigned to you at any moment.[12] And if you have already put enough aside to acquire livestock and agricultural implements, then you will not have to fork over a single penny for the land. This is because it will be easy to find a man of means who, in exchange for half of the league, will assume in full all costs associated with the whole league. Certainly an extraordinary advantage for the immigrant! He will then come into the possession of 2,222 acres of land for practically nothing, a quantity that will surely fetch a high price in ten years if immigration continues to progress at the rate it has begun, and there is little doubt that it will. There is also advantage for those who decide to assume the costs (the investors). To take an example, an unmarried man of means can only lay claim to a quarter league of land, but the expense of such is relatively higher in comparison to a full league because the costs associated with the smaller tract amount to $100 whereas they only amount to $160 for a full league. Also, a wealthy individual who already has obtained an entire league for himself and who therefore cannot apply for another in his own name will find no better way to put his money to use than to invest in this way.

Incidentally, an individual who is married and makes the trip over alone needs to search deep within himself as to whether he has the strength of character to endure prolonged separation from wife and child. Pain and homesickness can easily overwhelm such a person, and when that happens, he can quickly lose sight of his long-term goals and sink into inactivity and listlessness. Moreover, he becomes susceptible to unscrupulous individuals when unhappy and devoid of friends and a sympathetic ear. I have gotten to know several such individuals who found themselves in such a situation. I offered everything within my powers to console them. But they were so at odds with themselves, with the world, and with Texas that my efforts had little weight. As might be expected, the reports of such people back to Europe cannot leave a very good impression. Alas, some people are so nearsighted that they attribute the cause for their suffering to a country that is not at all to blame, but that is able to offer one lucky enough to set foot in such a place a promising perspective for the future.

Furthermore, I need to advise my countrymen to arrange their trip so as to arrive either in the fall or winter. They will then have the advantage of a year to acclimate. By not doing this, there would be a year's loss in the cultivation of the land. This is because if you are able to prepare a few acres in the fall for rye,[13] then you will be able to harvest in May. Incidentally, corn is usually best planted in February or March and is usually ripe by August. Also, everyone should take my warning to heart, and that is to ease yourself into the daily work routine, so as to grow accustomed to it by stages. For the average upright and industrious German, one cannot recommend this course of action strongly enough, because if he does otherwise the climate will surely do him in, especially in the heat of summer. But one should not fold his hands in his lap and do nothing. Such was the case with a certain O . . . sch family, who deceived themselves that all Germans were bound and obligated to work for them without recompense. Considering work unpleasant and beneath his dignity, the head of this household restricted his activity almost exclusively to the hunt, practically the only activity for which he was qualified in consideration of his previous occupation. In the meantime, a German who earned his livelihood with his hands was so crude as to demand the money he had earned by his labors, and doubtless in a manner so direct and unadorned that he was not led astray by the refined sophistry and arts of avoidance acquired in the fatherland by his employer and used for avoiding payment.

So when a complaint was lodged against him, this person took great offense that rather than providing a wide-open opportunity for chicanery, blunt Mexican laws unconditionally instructed him to pay, though at a rate benign enough for him to satisfy his creditor immediately. Enraged about this, the family vowed it would return to the fatherland immediately and give an appropriate account about this uncouth country, its cannibalistic inhabitants, and its entangling judiciary. It will certainly not be necessary for me to warn those of my countrymen, who think for themselves in any case, against such reports, since it goes without saying that they deserve no credibility.

I CANNOT REFRAIN from remarking further that the immigrating head of a family, if he in any manner has the means, should bring his family right away. If a man is engaged, then certainly his fiancée, if she has good intentions, will follow her love. I cannot but urgently and earnestly repeat this piece of advice, for no one obtains a full league of land if he cannot state under oath that he has brought his wife or family within the boundaries of the republic. All other kinds of evidence will be rejected as insufficient. Weddings are performed here by *alcaldes* (justices of the peace), there still being a shortage of appointed ecclesiastics. But there is no difficulty here in getting married; nobody needs banns, birth certificate, etc. The *alcalde* is paid ten dollars for the wedding ceremony; if that seems too much for some, they can be united in marriage in New Orleans, where a Catholic priest will be satisfied with a dollar, and—if you present yourself as without means—is obligated to celebrate the union as an act of Christian love.

SOME OBSERVATIONS CONCERNING THE QUALITY OF THE SOIL AND THE PROCEDURES FOLLOWED IN AGRICULTURE AND HORTICULTURE.

AFTER HAVING SPOKEN in general terms about this subject on occasion in the preceding, I now want to attempt to discuss more specifically the activities of local farmers and the manner in which crops are grown, so that the immigrant can take note of the activities awaiting him here, and to keep him from falling victim to the prejudices of many newcomers from Europe who presume to know how to do things better their way. In so doing, they have lessened their harvest considerably by not knowing the reasons why the Americans do things in one certain way and in no other; they fail to consider that there must indeed be reasons when the native farmer deviates from European methods. Such deviations are partly due to soil properties that are different from the German ones; partly, and particularly, they are due to the climate here. Land and soil may reasonably be divided into three groups: the first and best is cleared woodland, the second rich prairie soil of black color, and the third is light-colored sandy soil. The first-mentioned consists almost entirely of decomposed vegetal matter, formed since time immemorial by falling and rotting foliage and twigs. It is very rich, slippery in wet weather; it will stick just like our marshy soil and is shiny in the same way; it is black in color and of unusual fertility that does not diminish for many years. The second type, rich prairie soil, has almost the same properties and color as the first; it is found on the lower prairies closest to the woodlands and with a higher admixture of sand than the woodland soil, but otherwise it is of almost the same quality, except that it wears out faster, though it is certainly suitable for corn for fifteen to twenty years. The third kind is sandier prairie soil, found at higher elevations and of a lighter color than the first kind, looser and easier to work, but exhausted after about ten years; however, it is still more fertile than the very best German sandy soil. Fertilizing, which costs the European farmer so much time and effort, is not practiced with any of the three groups; instead, when a decrease in production becomes noticeable, another piece of land is selected, which is not difficult in view of the large holdings. Since rich prairie land is common in Texas, it is generally used for agriculture; admittedly, woodland soil is better, but the work involved in clearing and hauling wood is so laborious that there is no advantage to be derived; actually, in the time required for clearing one acre, ten acres of prairie land can be put in cultivation.

The procedure followed in clearing woodland is briefly as follows. After a suitable area is selected for a field, which should not be so low that it is subject to flooding during the persistent downpours in spring, but not too high, either, since elevated woodland is usually too sandy, the tall underbrush is cleared with axes and heavy hoes, the latter for brush and vines. After being hacked off, this brush is piled high to make room for the felling of the trees, for if the brush is cleared last, it would be in the way everywhere when the felled trees are topped. The trees, which average a good one to one and a half feet in diameter, are notched by axe, a groove being cut two inches wide and one inch deep all the way around so that the tree will die from not getting any more nourishment from below. The remaining small trees are cut by axe two feet above the ground and the branches trimmed; these are piled high around the trunks of the notched trees to accelerate their dying off. Branches to be used for firewood are cut in lengths, and the trunks split for fence posts or burned if they are not suitable for that purpose; at intervals of about three feet, fire is applied and kept going until the trunk is burned through; these blocks are either used for firewood or rolled together and burned. Once the field is prepared for cultivation in this way, it is broken level with a plow. This must be done very carefully, since the tip of the plowshare will easily get under the big tree roots and frequently break; then the plow must be stopped, pulled back, and lifted over. Incidentally, after a few years, the roots will rot, and the stumps can then easily be removed.

In the preparation of prairie land, the sod is broken—after being burned first, if this is done in fall—with a strong, sharp plow and turned over so it can rot. The following spring it is plowed again and, if feasible, harrowed to bring those grass roots that have not yet rotted to the surface. The roots of our local wild prairie grass are very hard and tough, so in heavy soil a team of three or four oxen is required; lighter and looser soil can be broken with a team of two. In one day, three-fourths or at most one full acre can be broken with one plow.

Fencing of a field is usually done with split logs of ten-foot length and about four inches thick. They are laid on top of each other, alternating in a zig-zag manner until the required height is attained, for which seven or eight are required per section. For fencing one acre, seven hundred to eight hundred logs are needed; for ten acres, three thousand logs; generally speaking, one log can be reckoned for every foot around a given piece of land. For fences, those varieties of trees are picked that are generally easy to split; various oaks, pines, and a few others are suitable. For the making of such lengths of fencing, including the cutting of trees, one dollar is paid per 100. One worker can make 100 to 150 per day. It is actually one of the hardest kinds of work here, and at first a European will not have much success; this is the reason why Mr. Ernst came up with an easier kind of enclosure, which in many ways is preferable to the other and can be built by anybody without prior practice. The procedure is as follows. Along the line where the fence is to be erected, two posts of about two inches in diameter and five feet long are driven into the ground at four-and-a-half-foot intervals and half a foot apart; to make this easier, they are sharpened to a point at the lower end and sawed flush at the other. After one side of the field has been done, brush is placed between these posts along the line and stamped solid; in this manner a solid fence results, which is strengthened even further after a height of four feet is attained, when for every nine feet—in other words, at every other pair of posts—two posts are placed above in a cross and hammered into the ground. Heavy posts are placed in the crosses, and above the fence two ten-foot posts are crossed in such a manner that the upper end rests on the crosses of the fence, with the lower ones crossing below about two feet from the bottom of the fence. This way it is impossible for the cattle to get close enough to the fence to make a jump, even though they do not shun a five-foot height. Nor can small domestic animals such as young pigs, etc., get through, as they do every day through the gaps of a rail fence or enclosure.[14]

A field laid out as described here is planted in the following manner. As Mr. Ernst already notes in his letter, the chief products of Texas are the following: maize, or Turkish wheat—here simply called corn—cotton, tobacco, sugarcane, rice, indigo; this latter item is still not grown much. Sugarcane does very well in the lower part of the colony on the Gulf; here in the upper parts, experiments have not yet been made, so I am not informed enough about its cultivation. Corn is considered the chief product by every farmer here, and the conventional procedure for planting it is as follows: after the field has been plowed, light furrows of about four inches are drawn four feet apart, beginning on one side of the field and running alongside one another from south to north. Once this is done, the procedure is repeated from another side, with the same intervals, plowing now being done from east to west, so that the field will eventually be all squares. The corn is planted in the deeper spots where the furrows cross, four or five grains being thrown into each one, which a second person, following behind with a hoe, covers with about four inches of dirt. After later plowings between the plants, the remaining open stretches of furrow will fill up automatically. If the soil is suitably moist and the weather is warm, the corn will come up in a week to ten days. After the first two leaves have developed, the rows are checked and excess plants are pulled, since only three plants in rich soil and just two plants in light soil should be left together; if need be, replanting follows. The young plants often suffer from too much moisture, causing them to turn yellow, and also from a black worm or caterpillar that chews on the root and may wipe out entire strips in many locations. The surest remedy is to kill them, which is not so hard if the roots of suffering plants are checked, since they are then easy to catch. About four weeks after planting, the soil between the rows is loosened with a specially trained horse and a light plow, and some dirt is piled up around the plants. Later, when the plants are about two feet tall, the whole area is plowed, and if the last plowing was from north to south, then this time it is from east to west, with somebody with a hoe piling up soil, if need be, around the plants and destroying weeds still remaining near the stalks. For the time being, nothing else is done. But right after the soil has been loosened up for the second time, the vacant intervals can be planted with melons, squash, cucumbers, beans, and other low-growing vegetables, which later have soil piled up around them. Corn is planted during the first half of March; later plantings in April and May are uncertain, since to fully thrive, corn requires a few heavy showers, that is to say one right after coming up, another at the time of the second plowing, and a third when ears are beginning to set. However, the rainy periods usually occur in April and May at the change of the moon; later on they cannot be counted on, which, as already noted, is why a planting done during those later months of subsequent dry weather will not produce perfect ears. These ears usually have a thousand or more kernels, and only rarely does the same plant produce two ears. Depending on soil quality, an acre will produce twenty to sixty bushels. When the corn is so far along that the husks enveloping the ears turn yellowish and the milky juice of the kernels has a firm consistency, the green leaves on the stalks are picked from the top down and placed between poles to dry; the following day they are tied in small bundles and stacked to be used in winter as supplementary feed for the cattle. This feed is more nourishing than hay, but it should not be picked in wet weather or exposed to moisture, since that will take away its green color and characteristic smell; it will also make it mildew. When the leaves are picked, the vegetables in between the corn now get circulation and grow vigorously; the ears of corn do not in any way suffer because of this, but are actually helped to mature. At the beginning of July the corn can be used for baking bread. Even before then it is a common practice, when the ears are semi-ripe and the milky juice is thickening and getting mealy, to put them in salt water to boil and eat them buttered, a dish that is somewhat reminiscent of green peas. Later on, before the kernels get hard enough to grind, the ears are grated on a grating iron with large holes, which produces tasty and moist meal. In August or September the riper ears are picked with the shucks on and kept in dry storage. Those immigrants who arrive too late in the season to put prairie land in cultivation for the following year—which must be done the preceding fall so that the grass roots can decompose during winter, since corn does not do well in prairie soil that has just been broken—will do well by clearing and planting a small area of woodland. Here it is better to plant later, since the soil does not dry out so easily. If the land has been prepared as noted above, but no team or plow is available, a hoe can be used to loosen up the soil somewhat in those places where the seeds are planted, that is to say, four feet apart. Once the corn is up, the soil around the plants is continuously loosened until it is eventually completely chopped up.

For growing cotton, the land is prepared just as in the case of corn, except that the furrows for planting are set six to eight feet apart, since these plants will spread their branches farther. The furrows should only be plowed from one side of the field directly across, preferably from south to north, since the sun can then get to the soil better. The seeds are scattered at random in the plowed furrows; in the most favorable instances, they come up after only four days, and the young plants are thinned out so that only one remains per foot. Later the field is plowed just as for corn; however, in this case plowing can be done closer to the stalks than with corn, which spreads its delicate roots near the surface, whereas cotton sends its woody and branch-like roots straight down into the soil. Thus a lot of soil can be piled up around it, which is also necessary since vigorous stimulation will cause the top to spread out and touch ground, which would ruin the cotton. Nor should the intervals be planted with secondary vegetables, since cotton continues to grow until it is destroyed by night frost and would thus deprive the plants below of circulation. Timing is not as important a factor as in the planting of corn, since cotton is a tough plant that thrives in any kind of weather; thus cotton planting can be undertaken later than that of corn and continued until the end of May. Cotton is a beautiful plant, with flowers resembling mallows, yellowish white when bursting, but turning red the next day. A single head may have several hundred blossoms with green capsules the size of a small chicken egg; when ripe they turn brown and show five to six chambers, with cotton pouring thickly forth in nice weather so that it is picked every day. A brisk worker can pick one hundred pounds in a day, that is to say including the seeds, which are removed separately by machine. The seeds resemble apple seeds, but are a little larger and rounder; the wool adheres firmly to the tips and must be separated. The blossoms appearing before October will still produce ripe wool. The later ones do not reach maturity; the hulls are picked at the end of October. Cotton is usually sold, with seeds, to people with machines for separation; the price for uncleaned cotton is two and a half to three dollars per one hundred pounds. An acre usually produces 1,600 to 2,600 pounds, the latter being the maximum attained here by a local farmer. This year Mr. Ernst experimented with planting cotton in between the corn; at first it lagged, getting too much shade from the corn, but later, after the corn leaves were picked, it grew exuberantly and now gives promise of a good harvest.

Tobacco grows very well in Texas, and with proper attention it achieves notable excellence. Cultivation follows this procedure:

in late February, seeds are planted in a bed where some brush has been burned prior to preparation in order for the ashes to make the ground properly fertile. The tobacco seeds, which are very fine, are scattered thinly on the surface shortly before a shower is anticipated, so as to have the rain gradually wash them into the soil. When the plants have about four to six leaves, they are transplanted about three feet apart in a well-prepared fertile area; they will grow readily, particularly if they are planted in rainy weather, and thus it is wise to wait for this, since it will do no harm if the plants to be set out are even larger. Later on some soil is heaped around them, and when they have about ten to twelve leaves, the tops are nipped, which will force the sap into the leaves so these will grow as large as possible. The suckers that will soon grow from the leaf axils and at the tips above are carefully broken off after a week or so, and shoots by the root are also discouraged. But once the leaves are large enough, one root sucker is left; when the old stalk is mature, which is recognizable by the lower leaves turning yellow or having yellow spots, the young sucker is cut off close to the ground, where it will develop a new stalk and is treated just like the original transplant. In this manner, three yields may be had for each stalk if the weather is but somewhat favorable. For further ripening, the cut stalks are hung next to each other in a location sheltered from rain and sun, which will give the leaves a light-brown color; next the leaves are removed from the stalks and tied by the handful in small bundles, which are hung across thin poles or on lines for further drying and then firmly packed on top of each other. In this state the tobacco is ready for further use or to be sold.

Sweet potatoes (*batatas* or yams) quite take the place of our European potatoes, which they exceed, however, in sweetness and taste. The tubers are placed in loose sandy soil, in which they thrive the best, and are covered about three-fourths to a foot deep. They should not be planted too deep in the ground, since the young tubers go down very deep and would be very difficult to remove if they are not planted very close to the surface with soil piled up high instead. Several plants will grow from one tuber. Once they are about two inches above ground, all but one are separated from the mother stalk and transplanted elsewhere. They are placed a foot apart in piled-up rows, which must have three-foot intervals, because sweet potatoes belong to the convolvulus family of plants, which spread their runners in all directions. If no more shoots are available for transplantation, a few vines are cut from the mother stalk, divided into sections with at least three leaf buds, and planted with two eyes in the ground, with the upper one to be the stalk. These cuttings will grow quickly, and they too will produce tubers to be used. Sweet potatoes are red or white in color and oblong in shape. The roots are white and rounded, the leaves rather deeply indented and, incidentally, have almost the same taste as the potatoes themselves. The cuttings can be planted until the end of June; the tubers are not planted before the end of April, and edible fruits on the stalk are rarely found before the middle of August. They are taken up in November, and after the tubers have dried out they must be covered with straw and leaves, and with dirt thrown on top, leaving an air hole so the vapors can escape. This cover is all the more important since the slightest frost will damage the sweet potatoes. Mice must also be guarded against, since they crave the potatoes. The sweet potatoes and especially the yam roots may grow quite large, and the largest are usually the tastiest. They are boiled in vegetable dishes like potatoes, or baked unpeeled in a pot covered with coals. At present, they are one dollar a bushel.

Rye does well in Texas. It is sowed in the fall, but thinly, since the stalks spread a lot and often produce up to eighty blades. It is harvested in May and yields twenty to thirty bushels per acre. If the land is plowed under again, it can still be used for planting corn or cotton that same summer. Wheat does not do so well since it is subject to so-called blight. Here they have only the summer wheat with small heads, whereas our German marsh wheat would surely do better, since the local soil seems better suited for it. Buckwheat, which in Germany often suffers from frost because it is so tender, would be very productive here and is successfully grown in the United States. No experiment has yet been made with barley, there being no breweries as of yet, though their establishment would, no doubt, be very useful; but whoever undertakes such a business would still have to bring seed for sowing as well as hops seed or plants, since both are lacking here. Oats also do well; for this it would also be a good idea to bring seed to plant.

There is only a limited selection when it comes to garden vegetables, because the Americans only grow what they are used to eating, and this only extends as far as peas, beans, cabbage, different kinds of squash, red beets, onions, turnips, lettuce, and carrots. Head cabbage is rarely found, because the summer heat makes the leaves go limp and keeps full heads from forming.

Melons grow in large quantity and to unusual size with quite excellent taste, particularly watermelons, which with their sugar-sweet cooling juice provide splendid refreshment during the hot months. In part, melons take the place of fruit, of which there is none here as yet, though a start has been made in growing fruit trees. Peaches and figs grow everywhere, and lemons, oranges, pomegranates, and pineapples also thrive in the areas near the Gulf. A variety of field peas with a long pod often containing eighteen to twenty red or white peas produces, whether fresh or dried, a very savory dish. On the cornstalks, kidney beans wind around and bear fruit twice a year, in spring and again in fall. Cucumbers also do very well. Our German peas must be planted as early as the middle of February, since the heat, when it sets in later, will discourage their thriving. Many plants have extraordinary growth; radishes, cabbage, turnips, and beans often come up only three days after planting and grow fast. Wild plums, persimmons, dewberries, tomatoes, several kinds of walnuts, and grapes are found everywhere.

Red currants, gooseberries, raspberries, and strawberries would surely do very well if, as noted above, somebody would only bring seed. The colony is still too young for anybody to expect to find all of our native bushes; the Americans do not consider cultivating such items, and the few Europeans have had plenty to do in setting up their farms during the few years they have been here. Consequently, there has been but little time and money expended on this kind of cultivation.

It is obvious from the above that it would be a good idea for immigrants to bring all sorts of German seed supplies, for although all essentials are found here in abundance and exceptional quality, the limited variety might not satisfy them at first. No doubt many plant varieties would, as a result of change in soil and climate, grow differently, whether for better or worse; however, the experiment is well worth the effort. It would certainly give countrymen so far from the fatherland great joy to have familiar creations growing around them in the New World; it would lessen their feeling of being so far from home.

THE AUTHOR'S RETURN
TRIP TO GERMANY.

AS INDICATED in the preceding pages, it was the author's plan to settle in Texas even at this time; however, the conviction that his family would be spared much discomfort by his presence and guidance, as well as the concern that the publication of this little book might be subject to many difficulties if not done under his own direction, prompted him to return to Germany. Because of its similarity to the journey over, a description of the return trip might not be of particular interest to his kind readers; nor does the limited space of these pages allow doing this properly. The author will conclude with the sincere wish that the preceding pages may be of use to his German brothers and asks that they be judged with indulgence. No wish to distinguish himself as a writer made him decide to publish his travel account, but chiefly the pleasant hope of describing an easier and more secure advancement to many fine German farmers.

AS I BRIEFLY add mention that on my return trip I set out on the [bark] *Theodor Körner* of Bremen under Captain [Johann] Harenburg, and owing to many contrary winds was only able to reach Bremerhaven after sixty-eight days, I cannot but give public praise to Captain H. and his fine officers; they not only fulfilled their regular duties in operating the ship, deterred not even by illness, but also showed all of us passengers every good turn within their power, for which I here render my most obliged thanks. Concerning Texas, I may be permitted to make the following brief observation. The reproach may be directed at me that my picture of the state has no shadows at all. In order not to merit such rebuke, I want to add a word about the illnesses prevailing there.

I have already mentioned earlier that on the lower Brazos in particular, a kind of hot fever and also the conventional cold fever are prevalent. In the higher region of Mill Creek where I was staying, these only break out when unusually hot summers occur, and even then they are far less frequent than in that lower region; they may perhaps be completely prevented if recent immigrants will avoid too much physical effort, especially in the noon heat. An emetic, and later some Peruvian bark, will make these fevers go away very quickly. Generally speaking, it seems to me that this latter remedy works much faster in Texas than in Germany. The remaining ill effects consist, at most, of itching and the skin breaking out; this will cause immigrants only a limited amount of discomfort in the first year or two.

As the wooden houses get older, some bedbugs or house vermin may also occasionally turn up; the safest course is then to build another house, preferably of rock; or, for the former pest, to wash the wooden walls frequently with hot water, and against the latter to sprinkle with oil of turpentine.

Beyond this, I would not know of any complaint to record, since nobody is likely to suffer from homesickness and that sort of malady if he brings his family. Moreover, since more and more Germans are now immigrating to friendly Texas, soon a little Germania will arise in this state, and every immigrant there will feel all the happier.

NOTES

1. Dunt inserted a footnote here that reads, "At least nothing had come to my attention in Germany up to that time."
2. Dunt's footnote in the original text reads, "At the time of my arrival here, the price was one and a half dollars, because it had not done very well the previous year; this spring it was also badly damaged by water in the lower areas on the Brazos."
3. An acre here is like the English one, thus about 285 Rhenish rods.
4. Prairie consists of verdant, treeless land; in contrast to woodland, it is partly level meadow or bottomland and partly hilly.
5. Land endowments, colonies.
6. Three English miles on each side.
7. This condition is now considered satisfied as long as a house has been built there, which the owner may authorize someone else to occupy.
8. Or the new, or upper, colony.
9. A Mexican brigadier general.
10. Dunt's footnote in the original publication reads, "In November 1833 all import and export of any items for Texas was declared duty-free."
11. Tariff on entrance fees.
12. This and the following two paragraphs are translated by James Kearney.
13. The text says "*Rocken*," but this is surely a typo for "*Roggen*," or rye. Otherwise it makes no sense.
14. By open-range custom, which held sway at the time, it was the responsibility of a farmer to fence out other peoples' livestock from his fields rather than the responsibility of the stockholder to fence his livestock in. Thus the "fencing" of enclosures, whether pastures or fields, was an all-important undertaking. Interestingly, the Texas Germans often found their word "*Zaun*" inadequate for the Texas experience and quickly incorporated "fence" into their vocabulary as "*die Fenz.*"

APPENDIX 1

Louise Ernst Stöhr

Anders Saustrup

———————————◇◈◇◈◇———————————

AFTER THE DEATH OF Friedrich Ernst at an unknown date in 1848, Louise, his widow, married Constantin Stöhr (or Stoehr), a store and tavern keeper in Industry, Texas, in early 1849. She outlived him as well. Louise Stöhr continued to live in or near Industry, where she died in 1888. Her gravesite is still found there. The location of Friedrich Ernst's grave is not known.

Not long before her eighty-fourth birthday, Louise Stöhr was interviewed by a reporter from Die Texas Post, a Texas-German newspaper then published in Galveston, and an article was printed prominently on the front page of the July 1, 1884, issue (vol. 15, no. 2, 699). Later that year, in its December issue, Der Deutsche Pionier (vol. 16, no. 9), a German-American magazine published in Cincinnati, Ohio, reprinted the interview, but with numerous unacknowledged changes. Except for brief editorial comments in the original as well as in the reprint, the present translation follows the original text in Die Texas Post.

Although the old lady's memory is clearly flawed, her firsthand account nevertheless throws additional light on early German life in Texas and gives continuity to Dunt's account.

The First German Woman in Texas

The first German woman to set foot on Texas soil is still living today at the advanced age of [almost] 84 years on her farm near Industry in Austin County, Texas. Her name is Louise Stöhr (widow of Ernst) and she landed at Harrisburg on April 21 [April 2], 1831, with her first husband, Mr. Fr. [Friedrich] Ernst; they had arrived there from New York [New Orleans] on the Mexican schooner Saltillo. To a representative of the Texas Post, who recently paid her a visit, she related the following most interesting incidents from her earlier life in Texas; and indeed she spoke with expression and accuracy:

"I was born July 30, 1800, in the city of Oldenburg [Ovelgönne], Germany, and at the age of about twenty [eighteen] years married Mr. Fr. [Friedrich] Ernst of Varel [Neustadtgödens], [Grand] Duchy of Oldenburg. In the fall of 1829 my husband made the decision to emigrate to America and went right ahead and carried it out. After a stormy voyage we landed in New York in the winter of that same year and presently established a hotel there, which turned a very nice profit. My husband became acquainted with the rich old [John Jacob] Astor, a fine and honorable German, who advised him, if he wanted to become wealthy, then to go ahead and start a dairy; for a few thousand dollars he would sell him a

Figure 10. The Louise Ernst Stöhr grave is located at a natural viewing point on the hill above the Ernst settlement in Pilgrims Rest Cemetery, established in 1861. Family members are laid to rest close by. Photo by Geir Bentzen.

ten-acre site on the East River, where Wall Street is now located, and give him time to pay it off little by little. Although I advised my husband to accept this offer, he did not listen to my advice; instead he decided, in February of 1831, to go to Mexico, and more specifically to the province of Texas.

"So we then embarked on the Mexican schooner Saltillo and landed at Harrisburg, Texas, on April 21 [April 2], 1831. At that time this place consisted of about twenty houses, or rather shacks; Houston did not yet exist, even in name; and because of fear of the Karankawa Indians who at that time inhabited the island, you did not dare land at Galveston. From Harrisburg an oxcart took us to the small town of San Felipe de Austin, situated about fifty miles west of there. This last-mentioned place had three or four hundred inhabitants, and among these we found a German by the name of [Christian Gotthelf] Wertzner, who was applying himself to the tailor's noble trade. So Wertzner is the first German man to set foot on Texas soil; he died in the forties [1852] at [Joseph] Biegel's settlement.

"So here we were now sitting at the very end of civilization, since farther to the west lay Indian domain; and prior to our arrival no white man had crossed Mill Creek. From here my husband made tours of inspection to select his land, and thus did he also get to the forks of Mill Creek, where Industry is now located; and since he liked this area because of its romantic qualities, its lovely water and woodlands, he consequently had a league of land (4,400 acres [4,428.4 acres]) surveyed by the Mexican land commissioner [Miguel Arciniega], who had his office in San Felipe. (The Mexican government made every settler a present of a league of land; he had merely to pay the cost of surveying.) About two hundred paces below this place where I am still living today, we then built a log cabin and established ourselves as well as possible. A few months later we sold a fourth of our land for ten or twelve cows. Now, at least, we had milk and butter; meat was provided by the abundant wild game, and a few bushels of Welsh corn, which we had brought from San Felipe, provided us with bread until we made our first crop."

In reply to our question, how far from her the closest neighbor was living, the old lady responded, "Well, Mr. C. Fordram [Charles Fordtran] lived a mile to the west of us; he is the gentleman who came here with us; to the north we had no neighbor this side of the White River in Arkansas; to the east on the Sabine River, and to the south in San Felipe. The entire region as it now appears before your eyes in every direction—covered with farms, settlements, and towns—was one waving prairie with thousands of buffalos and other game roaming about. For two years we were living like this all by ourselves in the wilderness; even the Indians seemed to feel too lonely here, for during the years of 1831 and 1832 they would visit us, just a few times, and, truly, as soon as they found out we were Germans, they even approached us in a friendly manner and several times returned our stray cows and horses in exchange for a little milk or butter. At that time there was no money at all here; only trade by barter was known.

"As a result of Mr. Fordram's [Fordtran's] efforts, the fall of 1833 did bring us a few German immigrants. Among them were the families of [Wilhelm Gerhard] Bartels, Zimmerschreit [Friedrich Adolph Zimmerscheidt], Juergens [Conrad Jürgens]. The following year, 1834, the following German families arrived: Chas. [Karl Konrad] Amsler, [Jacob] Wolters, [Robert Justus] Kleberg, von Röder [Ludwig Siegismund Anton von Roeder], [Wilhelm] Frels, [Carl] Siebel, [Friedrich Wilhelm] Grasmeyer, and others whose names escape me. In the same year the first company of Anglo-Americans also arrived in this area and settled about thirty miles to the north on New Year's Creek. In our immediate vicinity only four American families had settled by the fall of 1834; they were: Joe Robinson [John Robison]—eight miles from here on Buffalo Creek—[William] Sutherland, Capt. [William H.] Jack, and [William] Burnett. This heavy increase of white people made the Indians excited, and they now no longer approached in a friendly manner as they used to; instead they began to harass us by running off our horses and cattle; as a result a number of bloody encounters did take place.

"The first white man here to be killed by Indians was Mr. Joe Robinson [John Robison], the father of Col. Joe Robinson [Joel W. Robison] who is still living near Warrenton today. In the fall of the same year, 1834, the redskins stole the wife [Maria Theresia] and two children of Mr. [Conrad] Jürgens who had settled four miles from here at Post Oak Point. The Catholic missionaries were successful, however, in retrieving Mrs. Jürgens from the hands of the Indians; but the children were never heard from again.

"The year 1835 brought us the Texan war of liberation with Mexico, and since we did not feel safe here, we moved to the more heavily populated settlement at New Year's Creek. We stayed here until after the decisive Battle of San Jacinto [April 21, 1836]. However, upon returning to our home we found nothing of the belongings we had left behind except ashes and rubble. Nevertheless, to this very day the State of Texas has not yet done anything to compensate me, even to some extent, for this bitter loss—despite the fact that my husband served in the ranks of the Texan army, and I myself made every extreme sacrifice to support the cause of Texan freedom.

"At this time the country began to get settled more rapidly, and the years between 1838 and 1842 brought several hundred Germans here. In 1842 we had the honor of receiving a visit from the advance party of the German Immigration Society: Prince [Carl von] Solms Braunfels, Count Boos v. Waldeck [Josef von Boos Waldeck], and Count [Viktor] von Leiningen. These gentlemen had the notion of turning Texas into a German colony and establishing a monarchy here. My husband informed them that this would be a difficult task for them, since too much of a republican breeze was blowing here, and the neighboring American republic would never allow anything like that. From here they proceeded to Mr. Fordram's [Fordtran's] and here, if I am not mistaken, with him as mediator, purchased the tract of land which they later gave the name of Nassau Farm; the New Braunfels colony was supplied with provisions from there."

In reply to our question, how many members there had been in her family, Mrs. Stöhr responded, "Five children; three sons and two daughters. My eldest [youngest] son is Hellmann [Hermann] Ernst, and he lives about half a mile from here; he is sixty-three [fifty-six] years old. The two other sons soon followed their father to their graves; he died in 1858 [1848]. My two daughters are still living, and you see one of them right before you; she is the widow Wilhelmine Schröder and has eight children and more than thirty grandchildren; she is sixty-one [fifty-nine] years old. I have been living with her since Mr. [Constantin] Stöhr, my second husband, died. Caroline Hinüber, widow of [Louis and Albrecht] von Röder, is my other daughter; she lives near Meyersville in DeWitt County."

In reply to our question, whether she was enjoying good health, she responded, "I still have a good appetite and feel as healthy as I did thirty years ago; but my memory is beginning to weaken; events of the last twenty-five years in particular I cannot retain; but the first years of our settlement have struck roots in my memory so deep that I can never forget them. I can still see the Indians clearly before me, as they quite cheerfully killed and ate our only ox right before our eyes; nor shall I ever forget how the Mexicans fleeing from the battlefield at San Jacinto butchered our best milk cow."

On this note we bade farewell to the first German woman in Texas.

Caroline Ernst von Hinueber

Anders Saustrup

IN THE DUNT version of the Ernst letter there is but the scantest mention of the five Ernst children who lived to maturity, the eldest of whom was a daughter with the full name of Caroline Friederike Wilhelmine Dierks, known informally as Lina. She was born in the city of Oldenburg on February 2, 1819, rather promptly after her parents' marriage in the same city on October 25, 1818.

Caroline turned twelve at the time when the Ernst family and Charles Fordtran left New York and eventually settled in Texas. She died in May 1902 at the age of eighty-three after having lived continuously in Texas since 1831, a period of more than seventy years.

In May 1837 Caroline Ernst married Carl Ludwig Socrates von Roeder or Röder (1806–1840), known informally as Louis. After Louis's early death she married his younger brother, Franz Ferdinand Albrecht Ludwig von Roeder (1811–1857) in August 1841. His life was also cut short; thus by the age of thirty-eight she was already twice a widow. In February 1861, the month in which Texas voted to secede from the Union, Caroline von Roeder married a third time, to Werner von Hinueber (or Hinüber).

With two additional siblings, Waleska (1801–1834) and Joachim (1809–1834), who both succumbed to a quick death very shortly after arrival, the two Roeder brothers had been members of an advance party posted to Texas before the arrival in full force of the large Roeder and Kleberg contingency, which reached New Orleans on December 1, 1834, but then became shipwrecked on December 22 near Galveston Island on the last voyage of the schooner *Sabine.*

Shortly before their departure from Bremen on September 30, 1834, Rosalie von Roeder (1813–1907), younger sister of Louis and Albrecht, had married Robert Justus Kleberg (1803–1888) in a notable alliance that produced seven children. One of their grandchildren, Rudolph Ferdinand Kleberg (1874–1941), who had an academic as well as a legal career, became somewhat of a family historian. His identity is slightly bewildering: although he was the son of Otto Joseph Kleberg (1841–1881), he was nevertheless styled Rudolph Kleberg, Jr., or Rudolph Kleberg II. The first by that name was in reality his uncle, Rudolph Kleberg (1847–1924), lawyer and congressman.

In the first two volumes of the freshly established *Quarterly of the Texas State Historical Association* (1, no. 4 and 2, no. 2), Rudolph Kleberg, Jr., published an edited English version of a highly valuable account by his grandmother, Rosalie (Rosa) Kleberg, "Some of My Early Experiences in Texas." In 1899, in the same place and manner, he produced a similar account, "Life of German Pioneers in Early Texas," by Caroline Ernst von Hinueber, then almost eighty years old. That is the account presented here.

Caroline's brief reminiscences present a needed counterweight to her father's somewhat facile and pastoral description and, to a lesser extent, to those of her mother and Jordt as well. Her recollections are in many ways closer to the pungent vignette by Heinrich Pauck. Even at the remove of two-thirds of a century, a child's sharp perception of a life of deprivation and little cheer leaves a lasting impression without need of any editorial assistance or elaboration beyond factual matters pertaining to names and locale.

Life of German Pioneers in Early Texas

When my father came to Texas, I was a child of eleven or twelve [twelve]. My father's name was Friedrich Ernst. He was by profession a bookkeeper [postal clerk] and emigrated from the duchy [Grand Duchy] of Oldenburg. Shortly after landing in New York he fell in with Mr. [Charles] Fordtran, a tanner and a countryman of his. A book by a Mr. Duhde [Gottfried Duden], setting forth the advantages of the new State of Missouri, had come into their hands, and they determined to settle in that State. While in New Orleans, they heard that every settler who came to Texas with his family would receive a league and [a] labor of land from the Mexican government. This information induced them to abandon their first intention.

We set sail for Texas in the schooner *Saltillo*, Captain [Francis J.] Haskins. Just as we were ready to start, a flatboat with a party of Kentuckians and their dogs was hitched on to our vessel, the Kentuckians coming aboard and leaving their dogs behind on the flatboat. The poor animals met a grievous fate. Whenever the wind arose and the waves swept over the boat, they would howl and whine most piteously. One night the line parted, and we never saw them again.

We were almost as uncomfortable as the dogs. The boat was jammed with passengers and their luggage so that you could hardly find a place on the floor to lie down at night. I firmly believe that a strong wind would have drowned us all. In the bayou [Buffalo Bayou], the schooner often grounded, and the men had to take the anchor on shore and pull her off. We landed at Harrisburg, which consisted at that time of about five or six log houses, on the third of April [April 2], 1831. Captain Harris had a sawmill, and there was a store or two, I believe. Here we remained five weeks, while Fordtran went ahead of us and entered a league, where now stands the town of Industry. While on our way to our new home, we stayed in San Felipe for several days at Whiteside Tavern [James Whiteside's tavern]. The courthouse [town hall] was about a mile out of town, and here R. M. [Robert McAlpin] Williamson, who was the *alcalde* [*sindico procurador*], had his office. I saw him several times while I was here, and remember how I wondered at his crutch and wooden leg. S. [Stephen] F. Austin was in Mexico at the time, and Sam [Samuel May] Williams, his private secretary, gave my father a title to land which he had originally picked out for himself. My father had to kiss the Bible and promise, as soon as the priest should arrive, to become a Catholic. People were married by the *alcalde*, also, on the promise that they would have themselves reunited on the arrival of the priest. But no one ever became Catholic, though the priest, Father [Michael] Muldoon, arrived promptly. The people of San Felipe made him drunk and sent him back home.

My father was the first German to come to Texas with his family. Hertzner [Christian Gotthelf Wertzner], a tailor, and Grossmeyer [Friedrich Wilhelm Grasmeyer], a young German, at Matagorda, both unmarried, were in Texas when my father came. There was also a Pennsylvanian [Heinrich Thürwächter], whom they called Dutch Henry, and a Dr. Adolph v. Zornow, who had traveled through Texas, but did not stay long. My father wrote a letter to a friend, a Mr. Schwarz, in Oldenburg, which was published in the local newspaper. This brought a number of Oldenburgers and Münsterländers, with their families, to Texas in 1834.

After we had lived on Fordtran's place for six months, we moved into our own house. This was a miserable little hut, covered with straw and having six sides, which were made out of moss. The roof was by no means waterproof, and we often held an umbrella over our bed when it rained at night, while the cows came and ate the moss. Of course, we suffered a great deal in the winter. My father had tried to build a chimney and fireplace out of logs and clay, but we were afraid to light a fire because of the extreme combustibility of our dwelling. So we had to shiver. Our shoes gave out, and we had to go barefoot in winter, for we did not know how to make moccasins. Our supply of clothes was also insufficient, and we had no spinning wheel, nor did we know how to spin and weave like the Americans. It was twenty-eight miles to San Felipe, and, besides, we had no money. When we could buy things, my first calico dress cost fifty cents per yard. No one can imagine what a degree of want there was of the merest necessities of life, and it is difficult for me now to understand how we managed to live and get along under the circumstances. Yet we did so in some way. We were really better supplied than our neighbors with household and farm utensils, but they knew better how to help themselves. [William] Sutherland used his razor for cutting kindling, killing pigs, and cutting leather for moccasins. My mother was once called to a neighbor's house, five miles from us, because one of the little children was very sick. My mother slept on a deer skin, without a pillow, on the floor. In the morning, the lady of the house poured water over my mother's hands and told her to dry her face on her bonnet. At first we had very little to eat. We ate nothing but corn bread at first. Later, we began to raise cow peas, and afterwards my father made a fine vegetable garden. My father always was a poor huntsman. At first, we grated our corn until my father hollowed out a log and we ground it, as in a mortar. We had no cooking stove, of course, and baked our bread in the only skillet we possessed. The ripe corn was boiled until it was soft, then grated and baked. The nearest mill was thirty miles off.

As I have already said, the country was very thinly settled. Our three neighbors, [William] Burnett, Dougherty [Bryant Dottery], and [William] Sutherland, lived in a radius of seven miles. San Felipe was twenty-eight miles off, and there were about two houses on the road thither. In consequence, there was no market for anything you could raise, except for cigars and tobacco, which my father was the first in Texas to put on the market. He sold them in San Felipe to a Frenchman, D'Orvanne [Alexandre Bourgeois d'Orvanne], who had a store there, but this was several years afterwards.

We raised barely what we needed, and we kept it. Around San Felipe certainly it was different, and there were some beautiful farms in the vicinity.

Before the war, there was a school in Washington, taught by a Miss Trest [Frances Trask], where the Daughertys [Dotterys] sent their daughter, boarding her in the city. Of course, we did not patronize it.

We lived in our doorless and windowless six-cornered pavilion about three years.

When the war broke out, my father at first intended quietly to remain at his home. But the Mexicans had induced the Kickapoo Indians to revolt, and he was warned by Captains Lester, [John] York, and [Freeman] Pettus against the savages. We then set out with the intention of crossing the Sabine and seeking safety in the [United] States. When we arrived at the Brazos, we found so many people assembled at the ferry that it would have been three days before the one small ferryboat could have carried us over the stream. The roads were almost impassable. So my father pitched his camp in the middle of the Brazos bottom near Brenham. Here we remained until after the Battle of San Jacinto [April 21, 1836].

Thirteen [fourteen] men with their families, mostly Münster-länders and Oldenburgers from Cummins Creek, were in our party. They were [Karl Konrad] Amsler, Weppler, Captain Vrels [Wil-helm Frels], [Wilhelm Gerhard] Bartels, Damke [Georg Damp-ken], [Jacob] Wolters, Piefer [Peter Pieper], Boehmen [Bernhard Henrich Silkenböhmer], Schneider [Bernard Heinrich (Hon-ermann) Schneider], Kleekemp [Johann Bernhard Kleikamp], Kasper, [Caspar] Heimann, [Johann] Gründer, and [Ferdinand] Witte.

Some of the Germans fared ill on account of their tardy flight. Mrs. Goegens [Maria Theresia, wife of Conrad Jürgens] and her [two] children were captured by the Indians and taken to the [In-dian Territory] border of Texas on the Red River, where American traders ransomed the lady, but had not sufficient money to pur-chase the children. These remained with the Indians. The Mexi-cans captured Stoehlke [Reinhardt Stoeltje] and intended to hang him. Upon his using the name of Jesus Christ, they released him. Kaspar Simon was also made a prisoner, but released upon exhibit-ing his ignorance of the whereabouts of the Texan army.

After the war, times were hard. However, my father had bur-ied a good many things and had in this way succeeded in keeping them from the Mexicans. He had placed two posts a considerable distance apart, and had buried his treasures just midway between them. The posts had both been pulled out and holes dug near them, but our things had not been found. Our house and garden had been left unharmed, though those of our neighbors had been destroyed. The explanation of this is probably to be found in the fact that the Münsterländers, who were Catholics, had brought all their holy relics to our place and had set up several crosses in our garden.

Just as we had returned from the "runaway scrape," and had scarcely unhitched our horses, Vrels [Wilhelm Frels] came running up and told us that a party of Mexicans had taken his horse. Ellison, [John] York, and John [Freeman] Pettus, who had just returned from the army, galloped after the robbers, and, after [John] York had killed one of them, recovered the horse.

We had plenty of corn and bacon. My brother [Friedrich ("Fritz")] and John [Freeman] Pettus brought back a few of our cattle from Gonzales. Before the war, there had been very little trouble; but afterwards, there was a good deal of fighting in our neighborhood, especially about election time.

Figure 11. Friedrich Ernst established a post office on his property in Industry in 1837. This partly reconstructed post office stands at its original location. Photo by James C. Kearney.

A short time afterward, my father began keeping a boarding-house and had a large building constructed for that purpose. He tore down the six-cornered pavilion, over the protest of my mother, who wanted to keep it as a sort of memento of former days. Many German immigrants accordingly came to our house. Nearly all managed very badly at first, using all their money before they had learned to accommodate themselves to their new surroundings.

[The town of] Industry was founded about this time and named by Benninghoffer after a lively dispute. My father was a justice of the peace for quite a time, and later was engaged in general merchandising.

I remember very well the coming of the German colonists who founded New Braunfels and Fredericksburg. My brother Fritz accompanied [Prince Carl von] Solms [Braunfels] in the capacity of interpreter and guide. The prince had a considerable retinue of horsemen, dressed mostly like himself, after the fashion of German officers. Among the company were an architect, a cook, and a professional hunter (*jaeger*). Whenever they came to a good piece of road, the prince would say, "Now let us gallop," and then the whole party would charge down the prairie. The hunter was commanded to kill a deer, but did not succeed, and my brother rode out and killed one, causing much pleasure to the prince.

While on the same journey, the party stopped at a farmer's, who brought out watermelons and told them to help themselves. My brother cut a watermelon in two, took a piece, and went out into the yard to eat, whereupon one of the officers rebuked him severely, asking him how he could dare to eat when His Highness had not yet tasted.

When the prince was endeavoring to establish the Karlshafen [Carlshafen] (Indianola), and he and his party were making soundings, the boat grounded. The prince was in great distress and insisted that the only thing to do was to wait for the tide. My brother then took off his clothes, got out, and pushed the boat off the sandbank.

I also remember the prince's cook came to my mother for information in regard to Texas dishes.

I lived in Industry until I married [May 21, 1837] Louis [Carl Ludwig Socrates] von Roeder. Nearly all my time was spent in attending to our household, and I had little opportunity for traveling about. I was not in San Felipe after the war.

Wolters-Achenbach

Anders Saustrup

IN HIS MONOGRAPH *The Germans in Texas* (1909), Gilbert Benjamin (1874–1941) produced an English-language version of what is commonly considered "the Ernst letter," written in early 1832, supposedly to a friend in Oldenburg, and reportedly printed there in a local newspaper. The widely quoted letter has sometimes been represented as, and confounded with, the letter in Dunt's account; this occurred most recently in *Basic Texas Books*, ed. John H. Jenkins (Austin, Tex.: Jenkins, 1983). The result is a situation that needs clarification.

Benjamin did not view Friedrich Ernst as the same person whose letter he translated. He does mention "a letter sent by Ernst to his home," as a result of which "a number of Germans were brought to Texas" (p. 16). But to him that Ernst letter is altogether different from the one he translated and refers to as "an interesting letter by one of these early settlers" signed by Fritz Dirks (p. 17). Benjamin cited a book by Hermann Achenbach, *Tagebuch meiner Reise . . .* [Journal of my journey . . .] (1835), as the source for the Dirks letter, but in the process he contributed appreciably to the existing confusion.

In his introductory statement, Achenbach makes clear that he reproduces only extracts from the letter, not a text in its entirety (vol. 1, p. 132). This qualification is repeated at the conclusion (p. 135). Still, Benjamin represented his translation as being of a complete text and further states that because of its presumed unfamiliarity, "it is given in full" (p. 17). Of course it is not possible to give something in full of which you have only extracts.

If Benjamin had but called attention to the specific circumstances of the summary rendition of the letter as it is found in Achenbach's exceedingly rare work—no copy is known to exist in Texas—much confusion could have been prevented, and an interesting light might have been cast upon the particulars of how Achenbach gained access to a copy of the Ernst letter.

As the situation is presented, a German baker, Jacob Wolters (1797–1865), was in possession of the letter from which Achenbach was enabled to copy and paraphrase. Wolters was from Elberfeld (present-day Wuppertal), incidentally the place of publication, in 1829, of Gottfried Duden's highly influential book, *Report on a Journey to the Western States of North America*. It is quite possible to follow Wolters and his family as he pursues his determination of going to Texas and ends up, for all practical purposes, a direct neighbor of Friedrich Ernst, or Fritz Dirks, who wrote the pivotal letter. So Wolters is likely to have known, or to have inquired about, the identity of Dirks. This, in turn, would raise further questions, quite beyond the scope of this presentation, of whether a community confidence was loyally guarded, or whether the larger community knew Ernst was the author in the first place.

According to Austin's Register and General Land Office records, Jacob Wolters, age thirty-eight, his wife, Gerdtraut, age thirty-six, and their three sons and daughter arrived in Texas on May 7, 1835. On May 20 he applied for land on Cummins Creek (Sitio No. 3 on the San Antonio Road). But his title, issued in January 1836 with the Texas Revolution already underway, was void. After the birth in Texas of a fifth child, Mrs. Wolters died. Jacob eventually remarried and sired a second family. He continued to be active in the

Industry vicinity and met with a violent death in 1865 as the result of an accident. His grave is still found there.

What happened to Wolters' treasured copy of the Ernst letter does not appear to be recorded. It is even plausible that his numerous descendants are not aware of the direct role their progenitor played in its transmission. It may be mentioned as a tiny ironic twist that the name of this very Wolters—though in the form of "Walters"—occurs in Benjamin's study (p. 16) just before mention of the Ernst letter and his translation from Achenbach.

The Wolters-Achenbach version of the Ernst letter, as it will now be called, is obviously far shorter than the Dunt version by simple virtue of consisting of excerpts, contractions, and paraphrases. Still, it does contain valuable details, notably the exact date, which is not found in the other version. Short of new finds being made, collating the two versions will likely produce the most complete impression available of the original Ernst letter.

The notion that the letter was printed in an Oldenburg newspaper may not have originated with Caroline Hinueber, but it was apparently through her and Rudolph Kleberg, Jr., that it reached print and was perpetuated. No documentation has ever been presented or located for such a claim. Dunt clearly writes of copies being made—some of them unreliable to boot—as if this were all done by hand. Moreover, the Dunt version reads as if addressed to family members, not to "a friend, a Mr. Schwarz." But the family may well have had relatives by the name of Schwarting, a name that bears some similarity. It is possible that Dunt may also have changed the signature on his copy.

Because of infelicities, inaccuracies, and omissions in the Benjamin translation, a new version is presented here, including the introductory and concluding observations. For the comfort of the reader, care has been exercised to use identical phrasing wherever the Wolters-Achenbach and the Dunt versions are congruent in their respective wordings. Parenthetical exclamation and question marks are presumably attributable to Achenbach.

Right before the introduction of Jacob Wolters, Achenbach is engaged in conversation with an unidentified German dyer who has a hard time getting ahead even though he is almost the only one of his particular trade specialty in all of New York City. Achenbach's account continues as follows:

"In the course of this conversation [Jacob] Wolters, a baker from Elberfeld, also came by; he has been staying in New York for several years already. He, too, had not been able to get ahead in his trade and worked at one time in the shop of a fur dyer where he reported earning a dollar a day. He was looking forward to the speedy arrival of his family over here so he could move with them to Texas in Mexican territory; he was so taken in by this plan that he tried to win me over as well. To this end he entrusted me with a letter of a German colonist, from which I attach extracts here:

*Settlement on Mill Creek in Austin's Colony in the state of
[Coahuila and] Texas, New Mexico [Mexico], February 1st, 1832*

In February of last year we took ship for New Orleans on a brig. Even though it was still winter right at our departure from New York, nevertheless on the fourth day after our leave the mild air of spring was already drifting in our direction. Three days later, between Cuba and Florida, we had true summer, and during the entire distance of a thousand nautical miles across that part of the ocean, through the Bahama Islands into the Gulf of Mexico, right to the mouth of the Missisippi [sic], we were constantly working against the wind, which slowed us down somewhat. Going up the Missisippi [sic] to New Orleans, 120 miles (there are five English miles to a German mile), we received very favorable news about Austin's Colony in Texas; so we took passage again on a thirty-seventon schooner, which already had a hundred people on board, to go there, and after a week-long trip landed at Harrisburgh, in this colony. Every immigrant who wants to do farming receives a league of land in this colony, if he arrives with wife and family; a single man one-fourth of a league. A league is an hour's journey long and just as wide. In return he must defray 160 dollars in regular payments for surveyor's fees, installation costs, etc., must take the oath of citizenship, and after the course of a year is a citizen of the free United States of Mexico; as Europeans, who are particularly welcome, we, too, received a particularly good league and settled there.

The state [province] of Texas, of which our colony constitutes almost one sixth, is located to the south, on the Gulf of Mexico, between the 27th° and 31st° northern latitude. Followers of Napoleon have also settled here. Austin's Colony is traversed by the Trinidad, Rio Brassos [Brazos], [and] Río Collorado [Colorado] rivers; within it are situated the major seat of St. Felippo [San Felipe] de Austin and the townships of Harrisburgh, Brassoria [Brazoria], and Matagardo [Matagorda]; Tampico and Vera Cruz can be reached by sail in three to four days. The land is hilly and alternates between woodlands and native grass expanses. Great variety of trees. Climate as in Sicily. The soil requires no fertilizer. Almost constant east wind. No winter, merely like March in Germany. Bees, butterflies, and birds throughout the entire winter. A cow with a calf costs ten dollars. Everybody rides horseback. Oxen are used for plowing. Farmers who have seven hundred head of cattle are common. Major products: tobacco, rice, indigo (grows wild), sweet potatoes, melons of exceptional quality, watermelons, wheat, rye, all kinds of garden vegetables, and peaches in great quantity. Moreover, growing wild in the woods are mulberries, several kinds of walnut, wild plums, persimmons sweet as honey, and grapes in large quantity but not of outstanding taste. Honey is frequently found in hollow tree trunks. Birds of all kinds, from pelicans to hummingbirds. Game such as: deer, bears, raccoons, wild turkeys, geese, ducks, and partridges (these last-mentioned as large as domestic chickens), etc., in quantity. Free hunting and fishing. Herds of wild horses and buffalo; wolves, but of a timid sort, as well as panthers and leopards, but no danger associated with them;

abundant hunting booty, exquisite roasts. Meadows with the most gorgeous flowers. Many snakes, including rattlesnakes; every farmer knows reliable remedies for them. A league of land contains 4,444 [4,428.4] acres of hilly areas and valleys, woods and meadows cut through by creeks. With several settlements in one location, the value of land often increases so much that an acre has already been sold for a dollar. English language prevailing. Slavery prohibited, but tacitly tolerated (!). Daily wages three quarters to a dollar, with board. Items of clothing and footwear very expensive. Every immigrant builds his own log cabin. The more children the better, for the light field work. The way of life otherwise as in North America. Mosquitoes or gnats only common on the coast. For the time being no local taxes and later only slight ones. Hardly three months' work a year, no need for money (?), free exercise of religion, and the best market for all products at the Mexican ports. Higher on the rivers much silver, but still Indian tribes there (!).

We men amuse ourselves with hunting and horse racing. Because of a better market for products many people from Missouri have moved to here. From Bremen travelers should go to New Orleans; from there to Harrisburgh the fare is ten dollars per person; belongings are paid separately, and children are only half fare; you buy your own provisions in New Orleans; when the wind is favorable, the trip only takes four days. Because of yellow fever, travelers should arrive in New Orleans a few weeks before the month of June or not until after October. Once arrived in Harrisburgh, hire a wagon with oxen for St. Felippo [San Felipe] and report at the land office; very useful if you know some English; you only need as much money as it takes to buy the league of land and make initial arrangements. The head of a family must keep in mind that by being granted a league of land upon arrival, he receives as much land as a noble count owns, which shortly will increase to a value of six to eight hundred dollars, at which price leagues have actually been sold here many times. The expenditures for the land do not have to be paid immediately; many people pay the amount off in cattle which they raise themselves. For my friends and countrymen I have room on my property until they have located . . . [unoccupied] league, which does take time. However, Colonel Austin recently promised to see to it that such Germans as might arrive are to be preferably well situated. A man still unmarried should bring a good woman predisposed to country life; those who are married should not forget that here many children are considered part of your riches. Once arrived in St. Felippo, any of you should inquire about Friedrich Ernst on Mill Creek; it is thirty miles from there, and you will find me. In New Orleans it is advisable to buy a few axes for cutting wood, a pot for baking bread, as well as other necessary items at the place of business of [John H.] Martinstein, Rue de Chartres. This man is a German and will tell all of you what else you need. On the trip from Harrisburgh to St. Felippo you will have to camp in the open, so you should not be without some flour and meat; some rifles and hunting pieces, as well as a saddle, are essential requirements. The capital of Texas is San Antonio on the Rio del Norte [San Antonio de Béxar]. Your friend

Fritz Dirks

NB. Passports are nowhere required. Sons over seventeen years of age have identical claim on the distribution of land.

"So much for this excerpt which I here put before the public quite faithful to the letter. I do not believe, though it is extremely one-sided, that it contains any kind of factual untruth, inasmuch as other individuals who have already been there for several years, have reported the same and probably even more in favor of this region of the world. However, this much we know as established fact, that all of those objections which apply to the North American wilderness, weigh in even heavier measure on this particular paradise; and whether ultimately the easier marketing of products might not rather be impeded than promoted by the constant, bloody changes in the Mexican form of government, probably still requires careful examination before a decision is made to move to this state."

Nomenclature of Measures, Weights, Currency, and Other Terms of Designation

Anders Saustrup

----◆-◆-◆----

BEFORE THE U.S. government had struck a single coin of its own currency, President Washington, when first addressing the Congress (January 8, 1790), stated ever so hopefully, "Uniformity in the currency, weights, and measures of the United States is an object of great importance, and will, I am persuaded, by duly attended to." Though at that time efforts were already afoot elsewhere to establish rational standards beyond national application—indeed, as M. de Talleyrand later that year suggested to the Assemblée Nationale, acceptable to all enlightened nations of the world—it is clear that the world of 1790 operated with a babel of quantitative measures; those who for reasons of trade had to make exchanges on more than a local plane were confronted with a wilderness of conversion arithmetic. Though many of the designations—foot, mile, pound, etc.—might be identical, their applications varied considerably. This had changed little by the time of Dunt's travel in 1832, leading him to recommend, for example, that it was best to take along Spanish money when you go from a German country to the United States. In his book he also had to explain such now unfamiliar standards as poles and *varas*, leagues and *Morgen*, and compare them to their equivalents elsewhere.

To some it may be a source of amusement that the two major English-speaking nations—the United Kingdom and the United States—have remained the solitary keepers of such quaint, indeed medieval or premedieval, systems of measurement, which continue to be pressed into daily service in a much more modern world. The official English inch, for example, has been variously defined as (1) three grains of barley, dry and round, placed end to end lengthwise; (2) the breadth of a thumb at the base of the nail; or (3) the combined length of twelve poppyseeds. Consequently, there may have been some feeling of relief when on July 1, 1959, these two well-developed countries at long last decided they would finally have a common inch of 2.54 centimeters. This effort will supposedly produce some assurance that the average length of a barley seed, dry and round, is right at 84.67 millimeters. But others, less prone to amusement, will insist that merely giving themselves an inch is not enough to satisfy the requirements of the global village.

In 1824, during the reign of George IV (1820–1830), the Weights and Measures Act in Great Britain established the so-called imperial system, which went into effect on May 1, 1825. But when a major fire in London on October 16, 1834—the very year Dunt's book was published—destroyed the standard pound and damaged the standard yard, both in custody at the House of Commons, much confusion and uncertainty resulted in the English-speaking world. Up to this time, the United States had largely followed a variety of British models, but now, after the 1824 standardization, it decided to go with something old and something new. In measures of length and weight, the Americans stayed with the old mother country, but not in those of liquid and dry capacity. Whereas in 1824 Great Britain and possessions of the crown abandoned a confusing array of gallon standards (ale gallon, corn gallon, etc.) in favor of a single new gallon measure, the United States still follows Queen Anne's wine gallon of 1706.

The metric system originated in France as the most exportable product of the French Revolution (1789–1799) and was long referred to in the United States as the French system. It was successfully promoted during that revolution and was adopted there in December 1799, but not rigidly enforced. Emperor Napoleon I reintroduced old standards in 1812, and the metric system was not definitively established in France until July 4, 1837, when King Louis Philippe decreed it would become mandatory on January 1, 1840.

In October 1582, Pope Gregory XIII (1502–1585; pope, 1572–1585) introduced the calendar named for him to replace the Julian calendar, initiated in 46 BC by Julius Caesar (102 BC?–44 BC). It was quickly adopted by a number of countries, especially Catholic ones. In 1700 the Imperial Diet at Regensburg (Ratisbon) mandated the Gregorian calendar for the Protestant German states, with other non-German states, such as Scotland, following suit. However, Great Britain and its dependencies, including the colonies in North America, did not abandon Old Style (O.S.) in favor of New Style (N.S.) until September 1752. In that year, in accordance with Lord Chesterfield's Act of 1751, September 2 was followed by September 14. Thus the interval September 3–13, 1752, does not exist in U.S. history. The same legislation also followed Gregorian precedent by moving the beginning of the legal year from March 25 (Feast of the Annunciation; Lady Day) to January 1, a displacement still showing in the ninth through twelfth months bearing the Latin numbering *septem-decem* (7–10). As a result, fixed dates might or might not be moved accordingly, George Washington's birthday being the best-known U.S. instance. Thus the birthday of, say, James Madison, who was still living at the time of Dunt's journey, is March 16, 1751 (N.S.), but March 5, 1751 (O.S.).

A U.S. mint was established in Philadelphia in 1792; in colonial North America there was no mint, hence the prevalence and persistence of the so-called Spanish milled dollar noted below. The first official U.S. coins (copper and silver) were struck in 1792 and 1793, but the federal government did not issue paper money until 1861 and 1862. However, in the present United States, paper notes of one kind or another have been known since 1690, issued by various political and financial entities, and during the years 1732–1863 especially by private banks. These banks are the ones against which Dunt warns his countrymen.

All references to time in Dunt's book are to local time, also known as sun time, reckoned according to the meridian of specific localities. By the time of the Civil War, the United States had some two hundred or more time zones. Standard time was not introduced in this country until November 18, 1883 ("the day of two noons").

Because of political fragmentation, there is a great deal of variety in all standards in the German-speaking countries, with many sovereignties having separate issues and conventions. Only those designations occurring in Dunt's text are noted. The same applies to Mexican nomenclature and terminology, including those of political and social organization. Here the provenience is Spanish throughout. When, with the stroke of a pen, Yo el Rey, Philip II (r. 1556–1598) decreed on May 8, 1561, that henceforth Madrid would be the *unica corte*, a number of Castilian standards were already set and bear the cognomen of Burgos, capital of Castilla la Vieja (Old Castile).

There are no specific references to temperature in Dunt's book.

For further reading on references to measures, weights, currency, and other terms of designation, see the following sources: A. E. Berriman, *Historical Metrology* . . . (1953; repr., New York: Greenwood Press, 1969), especially 158–164; Colin R. Bruce II, ed., *Standard Catalog of World Coins*, 7th ed. (Iola, Tex.: Krause Publications, 1980), especially 680–683; Francis G. Clarke, *The American Ship-Master's Guide and Commercial Assistant* . . . (Boston: Allen and Co., 1838), especially 173, 215 in the chapter entitled "Exchange Calculations"; Horace Doursther, *Dictionnaire universel des poids et mesures anciens et modernes, contenant des tables de monaies de tous les pays* (Brussels: M. Hayez, 1840; facs. repr., Amsterdam, 1976); Bruno Kisch, *Scales and Weights*, Yale Studies in the History of Science and Medicine, no. 1 (New Haven, Conn.: Yale University Press, 1965), especially 18ff; *U.S. Census Bureau. Statistical Abstract of the United States, 1988* (Washington, D.C.: Bureau of the

Census, 1987), especially conversion chart, xiv; "Texas Land Measure," GLO-SD-01-(1–82), short chart of measurements and conversions (Austin Central Land Office, 1982).

Glossary of Terms

acre: A unit of area in English-speaking countries equal to 43,560 sq. ft., $\frac{1}{640}$ sq. mi., 0.405 ha, or 4,050 sq. mi. Used informally and inexactly in this text by Ernst and Dunt as equivalent of *Morgen*.

alcabala, Sp. (n., f.): A sales tax in colonial Spanish America, levied at various percentage rates (mostly 2–10 percent) depending on time and place; introduced into New Spain in 1575.

alcalde, Sp. (n., m., -s): A title of Arabic origin for an official in Spanish and Mexican municipal government; head of the *ayuntamiento* or *cabildo* (the latter term also used for the equivalent of town hall); in addition the *alcalde* performed judicial services somewhat like those of a justice of the peace. The title has no precise English equivalent. In Texas, members of the *ayuntamiento* were elected annually in December, with new terms beginning January 1.

arancel, Sp. (n., m.): A term of Arabic origin but uncertain etymology, likely meaning "a listing of valuable items" (*vide* Aniceto de Pagés, *Gran Diccionario de la lengua castellana*, I, 520). Commonly used in the sense of *arancel de aduanas*, i.e., official customs duties or tariff; more generally fees, taxes, etc., paid at the customs house.

bit: A monetary value first based on the Spanish milled dollar or piaster of 8 reales, also known in English as bits (at times coins would be physically divided); the usage was extended to $\frac{1}{8}$ U.S. dollar or 12½ cents, and is still so known in the vernacular. With further binary division, half a bit (6¼ cents) was known as a picayune.

bushel (bu): A unit of dry capacity; in the United States, equal to 4 pecks, 8 gals., or 32 qts.; metrically equal to 35.238 l. The bushel in German-speaking countries (*Scheffel*, n., m., -s, -) is a unit of enormous range, from less than 1 to more than 8 of its U.S.

equivalents. Thus the bushel of Bavaria is 6.3 U.S. bu (222.39 l), of Prussia 1.46 bu (54.96 l), of Saxony 3.04 bu (107.43 l), of Württemberg 503 bu (177.226 l), etc. In comparison, the Oldenburg bu is quite small, at about 0.69 U.S. bu (ca. 22.5 l).

cent (c or ¢): A U.S. coin and monetary unit, $\frac{1}{100}$ dollar; used informally and inexactly by Ernst and Dunt as the equivalent of the Oldenburg Grote.

Congress price: The price set by acts of the U.S. Congress for the sale of public land to settlers. In the Land Act of May 18, 1796, it was first set at $2 per acre; not until the Public Land Act of August 24, 1820, was the price per acre reduced to $1.25.

dollar ($): A U.S. monetary unit; the word itself ultimately derived from the German *Thaler* (modern spelling *Taler*), modified to dollar in England before 1600; used informally in this text as equivalent to the Spanish milled dollar (piaster, etc.) and the Reichsthaler.

foot (ft): A U.S. unit of length equal to 12 inches or 30.5 cm. In German-speaking lands more than a hundred standards have been known for the Fuß (n., m., -es, - or ¨/e), ranging from ca. 9.8 in. (25 cm) to ca. 13.4 in. (34 cm). Thus in Bavaria (since 1809) a foot was 11.491 in. (29.186 cm), in Bremen 11.386 in. (28.92 cm), in Hesse-Darmstadt (since 1818) 9.843 in. (25 cm), etc. Most widely used at Dunt's time was the Rhenish foot (adopted by Prussia in 1816) at 12.36 U.S. in. (31.385 cm). The Oldenburg foot is the equivalent of 0.97 U.S. ft. or 11.67 in. (29.64 cm). The Fuß was most commonly, but not invariably, divided decimally or duodecimally into 10 or 12 inches and called Zoll (n., m., -s, -).

Grote, Ger. (n., f., -): A monetary unit formerly in widespread use in northern German lands and beyond, but apparently (*vide* Grimm's *Deutches Würterbuch*, vol. 4, sec. 1, pt. 6, 591) only struck in Oldenburg and Bremen; in Oldenburg, 5 Schwaren constituted a Grote, 72 of which in turn made *ein Thaler* in Gold or Reichsthaler. In this text, a Grote is used informally and inexactly as the equivalent of a U.S. cent.

hacienda, Sp. (n., f., -s): A large landholding of five or more *sitios*. Within the Texas region this text discusses, the term seems to have been used only used in reference to the Cummins hacienda on Mill Creek.

inch (in.): A U.S. unit of length equal to 2.54 cm. In German-speaking countries, the inch (Zoll) displays the identical variability of the foot (Fuß), of which it is most commonly a decimal or a duo-decimal fraction. The Zoll would be further divided into 10 or 12 Linien (lines); it might range from about 0.86 U.S. in. (2.2 cm) to 1.2 in. (3 cm). Thus in Bavaria it was 0.955 U.S. in. (2.43 cm), in Prussia 1.03 in. (2.62 cm), and in Saxony 0.929 in. (2.36 cm). The Oldenburg inch was about 0.97 U.S. in. (2.46 cm).

labor, Sp. (n., f., -es): A regionally and internationally variable unit of area of Hispanic origin, conceptually based on the amount of land that would sustain a single family. An area of 1,000 *varas* square is a *labor*; using the Texas *vara* as a standard, a *labor* is thus 177.1 acres, 0.277 sq. mi., or 71.73 ha. An area of 25 *labores* is a *sitio* or a league square.

Last, Ger. (n., f., -): A German unit of measurement used for indicating tonnage of ships; usually stated as the approximate equivalent of 2 tons.

league (Sp. *Legua*, n., f., -s): As a unit of length, a league equals 5,000 *varas*; with the Texas *vara* as a standard, it is thus 2.63 mi. or 4.2 km. Widely used as well in the meaning of a league square, the equivalent of 25 *labores*, or 5,000 *varas* square. Thus with the Texas *vara* as a standard, a league square or a *sitio* is 4,228.4 acres, 6.92 sq. mi., or 17.71 sq. km.

manos muertas, Sp.: "Dead hands" (Eng., *mortmain*); here, a legal term for the practice of leaving a gift in perpetuity to an institution or corporation for religious or similar purposes.

mile (mi.): A widespread and variable unit of length originally based on the Roman concept of a thousand paces (*mille passus* or *milia passum*); as a U.S. measure it is equal to 5,280 ft., 1,760 yds., 320 rods, or 1.609 km. A German mile (*Meile*, n., f., -n) may range from 3¼ to over 6 English mi. (5.2 to 9.7 km). In Prussia,

Mecklenburg, and Hamburg, the mile was 4.7 U.S. mi. (7.53 km), in Bavaria 4.6 mi. (7.42 km), but in Baden 5.5 mi. (8.88 km). The Oldenburg mile was 6.1 U.S. mi. (9.88 km).

Morgen, der, Ger. (n., m., -s, -): A regionally variable unit of land largely used in German-speaking countries, conceptually based on the amount of land normally plowed in the course of a morning (*Morgen*). It was also used in Holland and the Dutch colonies (referred to as Dutch acre), and is documented in English usage as early as 1674. In Dunt's book it is used informally and inexactly as the equivalent of an acre. The *Morgen* may range from 0.54 acres or 2,168 sq. mi. (Mecklenburg-Strelitz) to 1.59 acres or 6,643 sq. mi. (Baden). Other instances are closer to each other: Hesse-Nassau, 0.62 acres (2,500 sq. mi.); Prussia, 0.63 acres (2,553 sq. mi.); Bremen, 0.64 acres (2,572 sq. mi.); Saxony, 0.68 acres (2,767 sq. mi.); or Württemberg, 0.78 acres (3,152 sq. mi.). In Oldenburg, the equivalent is 1.12 acres (4,538 sq. mi.). In German countries at this time, however, the practice of using the so-called geographical mile as a standard also became increasingly common. This is calculated as 1/15 of one degree of the meridian, or 4.6 mi. (7.41 km). However, even though Ernst and Dunt both refer to *Morgen*, this unit of land measure was not prevalent in Oldenburg at the time, except for the region of the Steingerland directly west of the Weser River. The very large Stedinger *Morgen* was 12,256 sq. mi., or 3.03 acres. The common Oldenburg area unit was the Jück (n., n., -e) at 4,538 sq. mi. or 1.12 acres, which, though never mentioned by name, should probably be inferred in these instances.

nautical mile: Originated as a navigational convenience based on the closeness of the regular mile and of an older sea mile to one minute of one degree of the equator of the earth. As a British unit (Admiralty mile), fixed at 6,080 ft., 1.15 (land) mi., or 1.85 km. The sailing distance from New York to New Orleans is calculated at 1,711 nautical miles; from Havre de Grâce (Le Havre) to New York (route of the Ernst family), it is 1,227 nautical miles. Further marine distances indicated in the text are New

York to New Orleans at 1,711 nautical miles and New Orleans to Bremen at 5,130 nautical miles.

peso, Sp. (n., m., -s): Also known as *peso fuerte*, eight reales, etc., but it occurs nowhere in Dunt's account; it is another term for the Spanish dollar or piaster.

piaster, also piastre, from Sp. *Piastra* (n., f., -s): The equivalent of the Spanish dollar.

pole: Also known as rod or perch; a unit of length of English origin, commonly used in practical land measurement, equal to 16½ ft., 5½ yds., 5.03 m. A length of 40 rods, 220 yds., or 240.7 m constitutes a furlong (furrow length). The common mile is 8 furlongs. As indicated by Dunt, an acre was frequently measured as 40 × 4 poles or rods (or an acre length by an acre breadth), equal to 600 × 66 ft. or 220 × 22 yds., thus 43,560 sq. ft. or 4,840 sq. yds. The long furrow and hence the long acre, normally of 32 furrows, was a preference occasioned by the cumbersome plowing equipment making a minimum of turns desirable. In the New World as well, the so-called Gunter's chain was in widespread use for this purpose. Originated by John Gunter (1581–1616), English mathematician and astronomer, this chain, divided into 100 identical links, which facilitated quick decimal or duodecimal conversion, is 22 yds. or 66 ft. long. In practical terms, an acre (long acre) was consequently equal to a rectangular area of 10 chains by 1 chain.

pound: A U.S. unit of weight containing 16 ounces, equivalent to 454 g or 0.454 kg. A metric pound is 500 g. The specialized divisions of the pound (*Pfund*, n., -(e)s, -e) in the German-speaking countries are not considered here, but only those within the range of the pound avoirdupois (lb. avdp.), approximately 400–550 g. Thus in Prussia the pound is 1.03 lbs. (467.7 g), in Bavaria 1.23 lbs. (550 g), in Bremen 1.09 lbs. (498.6 g). Oldenburg used the pound of Hamburg at 1.06 lbs. avdp. (484.4 g).

Reichsthaler, Ger. (n., m., -s, -): The modern spelling is Reichstaler; a monetary unit of German-speaking countries since 1566, and of complicated history; occasionally seen in older English as *rixdollar*. It is the same as *ein Thaler* in gold, the equivalent of 72 Oldenburg Grote, and is used informally as the equivalent of the Spanish milled dollar and the U.S. dollar.

Rhenish rod; from *Rheinländische Ruthe*, Ger. (n., f., -n): Modern spelling is *Rute*; at ca. 12.3 ft. (3.77 m) most widely used of the many German standards of this generic designation. It is cited by Dunt in a footnote for defining the equivalent of an acre. An acre would contain 284.3 Rhenish rods square, rather an accurate approximation of the number (285) stated by the author.

rod: As an English unit of length, the equivalent of pole or perch. In German-speaking countries the equivalent Ruthe, modern spelling Rute (n., f., -n), containing from 10 to 18 (German) ft., varied greatly, ranging from ca. 9.1 ft. (2.8 m) to ca. 17.4 ft. (5.3 m). The Rhenish rod at 12.3 U.S. ft. (3.77 m) was most commonly used at Dunt's time. Oldenburg had an older rod measure of 20 (Oldenburg) ft. or ca. 19.4 U.S. ft. (5.928 m) as well as a more recent one of 18 ft. or 17.5 U.S. ft. (5.335 m).

síndico procurador, Sp. (n., m., -s, -es): The title of a member of the *ayuntamiento* who is treasurer, notary, and municipal attorney. The post has no equivalent in English-language tradition.

sitio, Sp. (n., m., -s): Also known as *sitio de Ganado mayor* (place or location for large livestock); the Spanish term for a square league.

Spanish dollar: Also known as the Spanish milled dollar, piece-of-eight, peso, peso duro, piaster (multiple spellings), dollar, etc.; a monetary unit containing 3 reales and widely used—whole or in fractions—beyond Spain and Spanish America as unofficial international currency; in official circulation in the United States until 1857; used in Dunt's text as the informal equivalent of the U.S. dollar and the Reichsthaler.

ton: Used in Dunt's text only in connection with tonnage of ships, thus presumably the cubical contents expressed in so-called register tons, each of 100 cu. ft. net tonnage.

vara, Sp. (n., f., -s): Highly variable and widely used unit of length of Hispanic origin, conceptually based on the notion of 3 Roman feet (or Spanish *pies de Burgos*), ranging from about 31 to more than 40 in. (about 78 to more than 100 cm) and intermittently referred to as a Spanish yard. Undoubtedly the Castilian *vara* (also associated with the capital of that kingdom and known as the *vara de Burgos*) frequently commanded official rank among such standards used in the New World, but the standardization of the Texas *vara* at 33⅓ in. is unique. This was apparently arrived at informally among colonial surveyors at an unknown time and later tacitly acknowledged by the Republic of Texas without statute or legislation. It was perpetuated after Texas joined the Union in 1846. Nowhere else is the *vara* defined in this manner. For swift conversion between systems, it proved a considerable convenience (3 *varas* = 100 in.; 30 *varas* = 1,000 in.; 360 *varas* = 1,000 sq. ft.; 1.080 *varas* = 1,000 yds., etc.).

Early German Literature about Texas and Detlef Dunt's Place in It

A BIBLIOGRAPHICAL ESSAY

James C. Kearney

IN THE NINETEENTH CENTURY an extraordinary relationship developed between German-speaking areas of Europe and Texas. The gathering forces of overpopulation and popular discontent in Central Europe collided with an anachronistic and repressive political structure to produce a strong push. As Gottfried Duden put it in 1829, "the true proof that a country is overpopulated resides in the fact that the mass of the population can only be contained within the bounds of the existing social order through force."[1] On the other side of the Atlantic, the surfeit of good and inexpensive farmland created an equally strong pull. The dynamic proved irresistible to millions of Germans during the course of the nineteenth century. Texas first began to draw Germans when it was still part of Spain and continued to attract them throughout the Mexican, republican, and statehood periods, roughly from 1820 until 1850. The most notable effect of this relationship was that Texas became a prime destination for German emigration in the nineteenth century, so much so, in fact, that by 1850 one scholar estimated that 20 percent of the white population of Texas could trace its roots to Central Europe.[2]

Interest in North America as a destination for German emigration gave rise to a literature so vast and rich that it became a class unto itself. Growing fascination for Texas produced its own body of literature, which emerged as an important subset to the larger body of work. It was composed mainly of travelogues and diaries, but came to include even novels and poetry. And when we add to the list of published works the twenty thousand pages of official reports, professional appraisals, inventories, letters, etc. in the Solms-Braunfels Archives—the official records of the *Mainzner Adelsverein*—the sheer volume of the material produced by Germans about Texas in this time frame cannot fail to impress. It is beyond the scope of this introduction to offer a complete historiography of all these works, but we emphasize that Detlef Dunt's little book occupies an important place in the prerevolutionary phase. A short discussion of each of these pioneer commentators follows.

The world-famous German naturalist Alexander von Humboldt (1769–1859)[3] was the first to awaken interest in Texas among Germans. In addition to the monumental multivolume tome concerning his travels and scientific observations of the flora and fauna, meteorology and geology of South and Central America,[4] he also put together a separate book on Mexico, which at the time was called the Kingdom of New Spain and included Texas. Humboldt spent all of 1803 in Mexico. The following year he published an account of his investigations in Spanish. In 1808 he reworked the original composition and released it in a German edition with the title *Versuch über den politischen Zustand des Königreichs Neuspanien* [Essay Concerning the Political Circumstances of the Kingdom of New Spain]. The word "political" had a notably more wide-ranging significance for Humboldt than the usual interpretation. The book is in fact a vast, all-encompassing analysis of Mexico, which in addition to essays on the physical geography and the agricultural and mineral prospects includes a sociological and historical interpretation. Humboldt never traveled in Texas himself, but he interviewed several officials who had firsthand knowledge of the territory. He also consulted archival sources. Still, other than reporting that Texas was largely grassland inhabited by nomadic and warlike *indios bravos*—he mentions both the Apaches and Comanches—and consisted mainly of secondary and tertiary geological formations, which made it unlikely that there would be significant gold or silver deposits, Humboldt offered very little detailed information about the physical geography of the province. Indeed, astonishingly little was known about Texas at the time, even among the Spanish authorities in Mexico.

Humboldt did, however, offer an analysis that proved to be prophetic. He addressed the question of why Mexico was unable to furnish enough colonists internally to establish a meaningful presence in Texas and thus solidify her claim, which was still very much in dispute. (There were voices in the U.S. government as well as private speculators and filibusterers who felt that the Louisiana Purchase extended to the Rio Grande.) As it was, with the exception of the missions along the San Antonio River, a couple of presidios (or fortress outposts) on the nebulous and porous eastern border, and a few ranchos along the Rio Bravo, Texas remained essentially *desplobado*. Humboldt suggested Spanish obsession with silver and gold and an associated underappreciation for the agricultural possibilities of the New World lay at the root of this dilemma. He contrasted this attitude with the North American approach to territorial aggrandizement, which was proceeding in the first instance through agricultural development and exploitation. Moreover, the North Americans appeared willing, individually and collectively, to eschew the comfort and safety of the towns and cities and to endure the privations and dangers of frontier life, something the majority of New World Spaniards were unwilling to do. Also, the Indians of North America were less agrarian and settled than their Mesoamerican counterparts, which allowed them to be dispossessed and displaced more easily. Humboldt predicted (correctly) that the inability of the Mexicans to colonize and settle Texas would inevitably lead to a showdown with the rapidly expanding frontier farmers and land speculators of North America. And although he does not say it in so many words, the inference lies close at hand that the only viable strategy for Mexico to retain possession of Texas and other unsettled territories in North America, like California, to which she lay claim, would be to fight fire with fire, so to speak; to try to bring the seemingly insatiably land-hungry Anglo frontier farmers from North America into the fold through a combination of generous colonization contracts or outright grants of land to individual farmers and then hope that they would eventually become loyal Mexicans. It was a risky strategy and a fatal miscalculation, as events would demonstrate, but one she had no other option than to attempt. Germans became an important part of this unfolding drama in many roles, as colonizers, filibusterers, and commentators. For his part, Detlef Dunt's book was composed and released on the eve of this impending collision.

Humboldt also struck a theme that many subsequent German commentators echoed, namely that altitude could mitigate the effects of subtropical climates. Germany, of course, lies over a thousand miles north of Mexico (and Texas). Still, the heart of Mexico proper occupies a vast, elevated plateau that renders the climate more temperate than equatorial and permits the cultivation of crops usually associated with higher latitudes, such as wheat and other cereal grains. The hillier regions of Texas do not provide nearly as great a contrast in elevation as does Mexico, but that Germans were constitutionally unsuited for the lowlands and coastal prairies became an article of faith among many German commentators, with the concomitant observation that they were more likely to fall prey to "adjustment" fevers in the lower elevations and in the wet and swampy areas. Humboldt was the first to make this observation, but nearly all of the subsequent commentators repeated it in one form or another.[5]

Finally, Humboldt set a high bar for scientific rigor and accuracy, which later German commentators felt compelled to emulate, with the result that many of the subsequent German works about Texas are of first-class quality. A fair number of these works have been translated, but many remain inaccessible to non-German readers and offer, indeed, one of the "silences" of Texas history, to borrow a term from historian James Crisp.

Interestingly, Humboldt returns many years later to play an important role in the history of German emigration to Texas. In 1843 the *Mainzner Adelsverein*, the corporation of German noblemen responsible for settling thousands of German emigrants on the frontier of the Texas Hill Country in the period from 1844 through 1847, petitioned the Prussian government for a subsidy of one million Gulden. The government responded by seeking a professional opinion from none other than Alexander von Humboldt as to the suitability of Texas for large-scale German emigration. Humboldt advised against it, among other reasons, on the grounds that the interior elevation, unlike Mexico proper, was not high enough to mitigate the effects of the subtropical climate and would not permit the cultivation of cereal grains, which he regarded as indispensable for Germanic life. Consequently the society did not receive the expected subsidy upon which it had predicated its efforts and its financial woes began in earnest.[6] One has to wonder how the course of Texas history might have been altered had Humboldt advised otherwise.

The next German commentator on Texas of the prerevolution period to follow Humboldt was the ex-Prussian officer J. Valentin Hecke. Hecke had heeded the call in the great patriotic war of liberation in 1813–1814 when the German states rose up against Napoleon. He served as a lieutenant in the Thirteenth Silesian Infantry Regiment of the Prussian First Army Corps and participated in several major battles of the war. Although trained as a jurist, his war adventures made it difficult for him to resume a civilian career. His experience was a common one. Former officers by the hundreds from many nations now found themselves unemployed and psychologically unfit for civilian life. They tended to congregate in the major port cities of Europe, where they followed with alacrity the news of gathering winds of revolution that were beginning to sweep across the Spanish colonial empire in the New World, including Mexico, where their military talents might be put to use.

Several of the early German commentators and adventurers associated with Texas fit this pattern. The Long expedition, one of the early filibustering expeditions organized in the United States with the goal of enforcing a claim on Texas as part of the Louisiana Purchase, included several Germans, most notably the former Prussian officer Ernst von Rosenberg.[7] Johann von Racknitz and Friedrich von Wrede, Sr., discussed later, also fit this pattern. As for Hecke, he traveled to the United States in 1818, where he briefly associated himself with Joseph Bonaparte, former king of Spain and brother of Napoleon Bonaparte, who now resided on an estate in New Jersey that he had reputedly financed by the sale of the Spanish crown jewels. Bonaparte and his followers hatched a filibustering scheme of their own to liberate Mexico from Spanish rule and set Bonaparte up as the new king. Nothing came of their plans, and Hecke quickly disassociated himself from the plot. He returned to Germany in 1819 and published an account of his travels and observations in 1821 as *Reise durch die Vereinigten Staaten von Nord-Amerika in den Jahren 1818 und 1819: Nebst einer kurzen Übersicht* . . . [Travels through the United States of North America in the Years 1818 and 1819: Together with a Short Summary . . .]. Moritz Tiling, who wrote the first book-length treatment of the German settlements in Texas published in 1913, claims in the opening paragraph of chapter 2 that Hecke spent a year in Texas and was the first to excite the German nation about Texas.[8] He is wrong in both these assertions, but subsequent scholars have repeated the claim.[9] A close reading of the book reveals that Hecke never ventured outside the Middle Atlantic states, and he certainly spent no time in either Texas or Mexico. His discussion of Texas occupies a scant seven pages out of 240 and rests entirely on hearsay. But based on what he had heard, he praised Texas as a land suitable for German emigration and proposed even that Prussia attempt to buy the province from Spain outright. Nothing came of this request, and although the influence of Hecke has been overestimated, once again the national interest was drawn to Texas by a published work.

Johann von Racknitz (1791–?), the next commentator, was the illegitimate son of a German nobleman from Swabia. He was a most energetic and interesting man who spent the early part of his life as a professional cavalry officer in the service of various

German states and exited the service, similar to Hecke, a decorated veteran of the Napoleonic wars. He was interested in joining the Mina expedition, another of the early and misguided filibustering expeditions organized by adventurers and land speculators in the United States.[10] Luckily for him, he arrived too late to participate in the expedition, which ended in debacle, but undaunted, and dissimilar to Hecke, he actually traveled to Mexico and through Texas in 1829, where he became obsessed with the idea of establishing a German colony in Texas. He was able to secure a contract for the first of these ventures from the Mexican government, and so to von Racknitz goes the honor of being the first German *empresario*, although neither of his efforts came to fruition. The first attempt at a colony in 1833 near present-day Bastrop cascaded into disaster when the handful of colonists succumbed to a double whammy of cholera and yellow fever.[11] Most perished, while the few who did survive dispersed among the other colonies as well as they could. Undaunted, Racknitz returned to Germany and wrote a couple of newspaper articles and also a pamphlet in 1832 encouraging emigration to Texas.[12] He also published a book in 1836, the year after Dunt's book was released.[13] The book is in effect an advertisement for Racknitz's second proposed colony, which was to be located in south Texas between the Nueces and Rio Grande Rivers. The effort was essentially dead on arrival since by this point the Mexican army had been defeated at San Jacinto (April 1836). Racknitz continued to press for his colony for many years from both the Mexican and Texas governments, although it lay in disputed territory. Interestingly, he never abandoned his loyalty to the Mexican government. He was in Europe when the revolution broke out in 1835–1836, but ten years later he donned his uniform to fight on the side of the Mexicans in the Mexican-American War and eventually qualified for a pension for his service.[14]

In respect to von Racknitz, the historian Paul Brister, who seems unaware of the Dunt/Ernst influence, concludes, "Although Racknitz established no permanent colony on either the Colorado or Nueces River, . . . [he] did more than any other German writer to promote Texas as a land ideally suited to German colonization. . . . He published newspaper notices, pamphlets, and books advocating the settlement of hundreds of Germans along the Colorado and Nueces Rivers."[15] We respectfully disagree with this summation for the simple reason that both Ernst and Duden are associated with success whereas von Racknitz is associated with failure. Nonetheless, von Racknitz's name must be added to the list of important German publicists who planted seeds of interest in Germany that eventually blossomed into a phenomenon so strong that it came to be known as the "Texas fever."[16]

In general, the most influential of the early commentators extolling the possibilities for German emigrants to the United States was undoubtedly Gottfried Duden (1789–1856).[17] His famous book *Bericht über eine Reise nach den westlichen Staaten Nordamerika's* [Report on a Journey to the Western States of North America] gave a favorable description of the soil, climate, and lay of the Missouri River valley between St. Louis and Hermann, Missouri. Largely through the influence of his book, this area became the main destination for German immigrants to the United States in the 1830s, the decade when emigration from Germany to the United States began in earnest. His was the most popular and well known of the many travelogues and immigrant handbooks that appear during the period. But as availability of suitable farmland in the Missouri valley dried up and news of this began to spread by 1832 to the principal port cities on the East Coast as well as New Orleans, many fresh immigrants who had been inspired initially to make the move to the United States by Duden's book began to cast about for alternatives.[18] Talk about Texas as the next Missouri valley, so to speak, was rife, and many considered altering their plans accordingly. This was the case for Friedrich Ernst of Industry (and, by extension, Detlef Dunt). It was also the case for Eduard Ludecus.

Ludecus was born in Weimar in 1807, the son of an upper-middle-class family with connections to the court of Karl August, Duke of Saxe-Weimar. Ludecus grew up in the cultured atmosphere of Weimar, the center of German Classicism and the later home of Goethe and Schiller, as well as many other luminaries of the contemporary intellectual life of Germany. Ludecus was a good student and the beneficiary of an advanced education in preparation for a career in commerce and trade. His studies were successful, but after a few years he grew weary of life behind a desk and resolved to immigrate to the United States. He collected letters of introduction, gathered his savings, and departed. In the course of his travels he regularly wrote letters to his father, who collected and published them in 1836. Perhaps they were intended for publication all along, since many commentators of the period made use of the epistolary style, including Gottfried Duden.

Ludecus was initially drawn to the Missouri settlements, but while in New York he made the acquaintance of Dr. John Charles Beales, a physician originally from Scotland, who convinced him to join his proposed colony in Texas. Beales had secured a colonization contract in 1830 from the Mexican authorities for a consortium of investors who called themselves the Rio Grande and Texas Land Company. The company proposed to settle up to eight hundred families in their grant area along the middle reaches of the Rio Grande at the point where Las Moras Creek empties into the river above present Eagle Pass. Beales arrived with a contingent of forty families in December 1833, and after many trials and tribulations the small group finally arrived at their destination. They found a semi-arid landscape covered with thorny brush, infested with snakes, and astride one of the principal corridors into Mexico used by Comanche war parties on their periodic raids. Despite a heroic determination on the part of the colonists to clear the land and dig irrigation canals, the effort was doomed to failure. The war of 1835–1836 was the last straw. The Ludecus letters compiled and published by his father in 1836 document the whole debacle and are invaluable historically on a number of counts.[19] Ludecus was a keen observer with a broad humanist background that informs his observations. The effect of his book, however, was sobering and hardly encouraging for future German emigration to Texas. In fact, the Ludecus experience, which was contemporaneous with Ernst and Dunt, provides an interesting counterpoint to the Ernst/Dunt enthusiasm.

Friedrich von Wrede, Sr. (1786–1845) is one of the most interesting German emigrants to have left his mark on Texas. In his later
years he became an official of the *Mainzner Adelsverein* in Texas
and a trusted troubleshooter for Prince Solms-Braunfels during
his tenure as commissioner-general of the society in Texas, 1844–
1845. In this capacity he was murdered by a band of renegade Waco
Indians at Live Oak Springs south of Austin in the fall of 1845.
We are concerned, however, with his earlier experiences in Texas.
Similar to Hecke, he was a former officer who had participated in
the Battle of Waterloo. He was very restless and traveled back and
forth between New Orleans and Texas on several occasions prior
to the outbreak of hostilities, and thereafter. He was a jack-of-all-
trades but seems to have supported himself mainly as a master of
dressage. His travels brought him into contact with both Friedrich
Ernst and Friedrich Detlef Jordt, aka Detlef Dunt, in 1836. He acquired land on Cummins Creek in Colorado County in 1837 but
never settled it. Eventually he did a land swap with one of the sons
of Jordt. Von Wrede published sketches from these years of wandering in 1844 as *Lebensbilder aus den Vereinigten Staaten von Nordamerika und Texas* [Life-Sketches from the United States of North
America and Texas].[20] The book, although published considerably
later than the Dunt book, nevertheless deals with the same time
period and complements Dunt's observations in many respects.

The details of Friedrich Ernst's life and the path that brought
him to Texas are to be found in the introduction. For the present
discussion, we note that many consider Friedrich Ernst to be the
father of German emigration to Texas. We agree with this assess-
ment to the extent that it applies to south-central Texas, one of the
two main areas of German emigration, the other being the Texas
Hill Country. Roughly speaking, the Hill Country settlements resulted from organized and sponsored emigration that began as at-
tempts to settle land grant contracts obtained in 1842 from the
Republic of Texas by the *empresarios* Henri Castro and Henry Francis Fisher,[21] whereas the south-central settlements resulted from
the process known as "chain emigration." Accordingly, a dominant

personality writes back to friends and family to start the ball rolling. The Ernst letter provided the first link in this chain, and Detlef Dunt, who came to Texas to see for himself if Ernst's glowing assessments were true, amplified the effect of his letter through his 1834 book with a resounding "yes."[22] Thus, although Ernst never published his own observations, the sensation they created and the verification they received through Dunt guarantees Ernst a premier place among the panoply of early commentators.

The division of the two principal areas of German emigration is an important distinction that also has a bearing on immigrant literature. The Hill Country settlements differed fundamentally from their south-central counterparts. They provided a true frontier experience in an isolated and exotic setting. The inherent drama in these facts, coupled with the sheer improbability that the whole venture was organized and underwritten by a group of German noblemen, generated much more press for the Hill Country settlements, both at the time and subsequently. Consequently, after (say) 1843, the majority of Texas literature focuses on the Hill Country settlements. But in the shadows, so to speak, the south-central communities in Colorado, Austin, and Fayette Counties[23] continued to grow and flourish, eventually achieving an immigrant population every bit as sizable as their Hill Country counterpart and one that successfully made the transition to new home and community. And therein lies the significance of the Dunt book, for it is an important component to this quiet success story. Dunt/Jordt was not an everyman in that his financial resources were clearly above the average.[24] Still, he counts as an important advocate for the common man who intended to make a new life for himself and his family in Texas on his own initiative and nickel and not within the structure and security of an organized effort. Among the early commentators we have surveyed, he was the earliest and most successful in serving this goal. And he was also one who followed his own advice and moved with his family to the Frelsburg community in northern Colorado County.

NOTES

1. Gottfried Duden, *Bericht über eine Reise nach den westlichen Staaten Norda-merika's und eine mehrjährigen Aufenthalt zm Missouri in den Jahren, 1824, 25, 26, 27* (St. Gallen, 1832), x.

2. Relying on census data and population estimates in newspapers, historian Gilbert Benjamin claims that roughly thirty thousand Germans inhabited Texas in 1850, accounting for one-fifth of the Caucasian population. See Gilbert Benjamin, *The Germans in Texas: A Study in Immigration* (Austin: Jenkins, 1974), 59.

3. Next to Napoleon, Humboldt was arguably the most famous man in Europe in the nineteenth century.

4. Humboldt traveled extensively in Latin America between 1799 and 1803, exploring and describing it for the first time from a modern scientific point of view. His description of the journey was composed in French and published in an enormous set of volumes over twenty-one years. He spent 1803 in Mexico, and his book on Mexico was published in German separately from the other work.

5. Thus J. Valentin Hecke wrote in 1818, "The interior climate is temperate and healthy because of the many mountains." Hecke, *Reise durch die Vereinigten Staaten, von Nord-Amerika in den Jahren 1818 und 1819: Nebst einer kurzen Uebersicht der neusten Ereignisse auf dem Kriess-Schauplatz im Süd-Amerika und West-Indien* (Berlin: A. W. Schade/G. Hayden, 1820–1821) 195 [translation by author].

6. For a discussion of this, see Kearney, *Nassau Plantation: The Evolution of a Texas-German Slave Plantation* (Denton: University of North Texas Press, 2010), 56.

7. The Long expedition of 1821 ended in a debacle when many of its vanguard were captured at the La Bahia presidio near Goliad. James Long, the leader of the expedition, was eventually executed. Ernst von Rosenberg went on to join various armies in the fight for independence that began in 1821 in Mexico. He was said to have eventually faced a firing squad. In 1850 his younger brother Peter Carl von Rosenberg, also a veteran of the Battle of Waterloo, emigrated to Texas with his extended family and settled at Nassau Plantation in northern Fayette County. His family became very prominent as educators and professional people in the state.

8. Moritz Tiling, *History of the German Element in Texas from 1820–1850* (Houston: M. Tiling, 1913), 7.

9. See, for instance, George J. Morgenthaler, *Promised Land: Solms, Castro, and Sam Houston's Colonization Contracts* (College Station: Texas A&M University Press, 2009).

10. The Mina expedition was organized in the United States and launched in the spring of 1817 by Francesco Xavier Mina, a Spanish citizen, who aimed

to overthrow the forces of King Ferdinand VII of Spain. After some initial successes, the effort collapsed and Mina was executed.

11. Louis E. Brister, "Johann von Racknitz: German Empresario and Soldier of Fortune in Texas and Mexico, 1832–1848," *Southwestern Historical Quarterly* 99 (July 1995): 50.

12. Ibid., 59.

13. Johann von Racknitz, *Kurze und getreue Belehrung für deutsche und schweizerische Auswanderer, welche an der Begründung der Colonie von Racknitz, im mexicanischen Freistaate Tamaulipas gelegen, Theil nehmen wollen, in Beziehung auf die natürliche Beschaffenheit des Staates, seine Verfassung, die bestehenden Verträge mit der Regierung, die Colonie-Gesetze, und die Aufnahme-Bedingungen in den Verein* [A short and true instruction for German and Swiss emigrants who want to take part in the founding of the von Racknitz Colony in the Mexican state of Tamaulipas in reference to the natural geography of the state, its constitution, the existing treaties with the government, the colonial regulations and the conditions for acceptance into the society] (Stuttgart: Imle und Krause, 1836).

14. Brister, "Racknitz."

15. Ibid.

16. Friedrich Armand Strubberg, aka "Dr. Schubbert," served as the first colonial director of Fredericksburg, a town established by the *Mainzner Adelsverein*, also known as the Society for the Protection of German Emigrants in Texas, in 1846. He later wrote a series of adventure novels based on his experiences in Texas. In several of these novels, Strubberg wrote of the phenomenon of "Texas Fever." For a fuller discussion see the introduction to *Friedrichsburg: Colony of the German Fürstenverein* (Austin: University of Texas Press, 2012) by James C. Kearney.

17. By early we mean the period from roughly 1829 until 1835. Thereafter, Traugott Bromme's travelogues and guidebooks claim this distinction. His first book appeared in 1835 and went through many editions and printings, the last appearing in 1854.

18. Achenbach cites an example of this in the case of Jacob Wolters, a baker from Elberfeldt who had been influenced to emigrate by the Duden book but changed his mind when he heard about Texas in New York and came upon a copy of the Ernst letter, which he shared with Jordt/Dunt, who reproduced it in his book.

19. Professor Louis E. Brister has produced an excellent annotated translation of the Ludecus letters: *John Charles Beales's Rio Grande Colony: Letters by Eduard Ludecus, a German Colonist, to Friends in Germany in 1833–1834, Recounting His Journey, Trials, and Observations in Early Texas* (Austin: Texas State Historical Association, 2008).

20. Chester Geue has provided an excellent translation of the book: *Sketches of Life in the United States of North America and Texas* (Waco, TX: Texian Press, 1970).

21. Fisher, of course, eventually sold an interest in his grant to the *Mainzner Adelsverein* or Society for the Protection of German Emigrants in Texas.

22. Ernst's letter was also reproduced in another travelogue of the period, namely *Reiseabenteuer und Begebenheiten in Nord-Amerika im Jahre 1833 . . .* [Adventures and incidents of travel in North America in 1833], by Hermann Achenbach, p. 132 ff. Achenbach cites an example of the letter's influence in the case of Jacob Wolters. The Wolters family settled in the Cummins Creek community (present-day Frelsburg) in northern Colorado County. The family subsequently became prominent in business and civic matters, and descendants still reside in the area.

23. And to a lesser extent Washington and Lavaca Counties.

24. For instance, he had the financial means to travel back and forth to Germany several times.

Chronological Bibliography of Nineteenth-Century German Works That Discuss or Mention Texas

James C. Kearney

1808

Humboldt, Alexander von. *Ein Versuch über den politischen Zustand des Königreiches Neuspanien.* Stuttgart: Gota'schen Verlag, 1808.

1821

Hecke, J. Valentin. *Reise durch die Vereinigten Staaten von Nord-Amerika in den Jahren 1818 und 1819: Nebst einer kurzen Uebersicht der neuesten Ereignisse auf dem Kriegs-Schauplatz in Süd-Amerika und West-Indien.* Berlin: printed by A. W. Schade (vol. 1) and G. Hayden (vol. 2) for H. Ph. Petri, 1820–1821. Vol. 2 is entitled *Reise durch die Vereinigten Staaten von Nord-Amerika und Rückreise durch England. Nebst einer Schilderung der Revolutions-Helden, und des ehemaligen und gegenwärtigen Zustandes von St. Domingo.*

1832

Duden, Gottfried. *Bericht über eine Reise nach den westlichen Staaten Nordamerika's und eine mehrjährigen Aufenthalt am Missouri in den Jahren, 1824, 25, 26, 27.* St. Gallen, 1832.

Racknitz, Johann von.

―――. *Vorläufer für Auswanderer nach dem Staate Texas.* Meersburg: n.p., 1832. [pamphlet]

―――. *Wegweiser für Auswanderer nach Amerika.* Stuttgart: n.p., 1832. [pamphlet]

1834

Dunt, Detlef. *Reise nach Texas, nebst Nachrichten von diesem Lande; für Deutsche, welche nach Amerika zu gehen beabsichtigen.* Bremen: Carl W. Wiehe, 1834.

1835

Achenbach, Hermann. *Reiseabentheuer und Begenbenheiten in Nord-Amerika im Jahre 1833; kein Roman sondern ein Lehr- und Lesebuch für Auswanderungslustige und gemütliche Leser.* Düsseldorf: printed at cost of author by G. H. Beyer and Co., 1835. [Reproduces Ernst letter, p. 132 ff.]

1836

Racknitz, Johann von. *Kurze und getreue Belehrung für deutsche und schweizerische Auswanderer, welche an der Begründubg der Colonie von Racknitz, im mexicanishen Freistaate Tamaulipas gelegen, Theil nehmen wollen, in Beziehung auf die natürliche Beschaffenheit des Staates, seine Verfqssung, die bestenhenden Verträge mit der Regierung, die Colonie-Gesetze, und die Aufnahme-Bedingungen in den Verein.* Stuttgart: Imle und Krause, 1836.

1837

Ludecus, Eduard. *Reise durch die Mexikanischen Provinzen Tamualipas, Cohahuila, und Texas im Jahre 1834 in Briefen an seine Freunde.* Leipzig: Joh. Friedr. Hartknoch, 1837.

1841

Scherpf, G. A. *Entstehungsgeschichte und gegendwärtiger Zustand des neuen Staates Texas.* Augsburg, 1841.

Sealsfield, Charles (Karl Postl). *Das Kajütenbuch oder nationale Charakteristiken.* 2 vols. Zurich, 1841.

———. Life in the New World; or Sketches of American Society. Translated by G. C. Mackay. New York: J. Winchester, 1844.

1843

Ehrenberg, Hermann. *Texas und Seine Revolution.* Leipzig: Otto Wigand, 1843. Subsequently published as *Der Freiheitskampf in Texas im Jahre 1836* (1844) and *Fahrten und Schicksale eines Deutschen in Texas* (1845).

1844

Berghaus, Heinrich. "Der Freistaat Texas." In *Allgemeine Länder und Völkerkunde.* Stuttgart: Hoffmann, 1844.

Höhne, Friedrich. *Wahn und Überzeugung, Reise des Kupferschmiedemeisters Friedrich Höhne in Weimar über Bremen nach Nordamerika und Texas in den Jahren 1839, 1840 und 1841.* Weimar: Wilhelm Hoffmann, 1844.

Treskow, A. v. *Ein Handbuch für Auswanderer, Mit Besonderer Berücksichtigung derer, welche ihre Überfahrt zur Ansiedlung durch Vermittelung des Vereins zum Schutze dt Aus. bewerkstelligen wollen.* [See SBAt I, 222, letter of November, 29, 1844.]

Wrede, Friedrich von, Sr. *Lebensbilder aus den Vereinigten Staaten von Nordamerika und Texas.* Kassel: Emil Drescher, 1844. Translated and edited over one hundred years later by Chester W. Geue, with the title *Sketches of Life in the United States of North America and Texas* (Waco, TX: Texian Press, 1970).

1845

Büttner, Johann G. *Briefe aus und Über Amerika, oder Beiträge zu einer richtigen Kentniss der Vereinigten Staaten von Nordamerika und ihrer Bewohner.* Dresden und Leipzig, 1845.

Eggerling, H. W. C. *Beschreibung der Vereinigten Staaten von Nordamerika mit besonderer Berücksichtigung deutscher Ansiedlungen daselbst.* Hildesheim, 1845? nicht eingesehen. Erwähnt in der

Hildesheimer Zeitung. 10.6.1845. Frühere Ausgabe: Wiesbaden, 1832.

Kennedy, William. *The Rise, Progress and Prospects of the Republic of Texas.* London: R. Hasings, 1841. The first German-language edition, translated by Otto von Czarnowsky, appeared as *Geographie, Naturgeschichte und Topographie von Texas.* Frankfurt am Main: David Sauerländer, 1845.

1846

Anonymous. *Der Auswanderer nach Texas: Ein Handbuch und Rathgeber für die, welche sich in Texas ansiedeln wollen.* Bremen: n.p., 1846.

Beyer, Moritz. *Das Auswanderungsbuch oder ein Führer und Rathgeber bei der Auswanderung nach Nordamerika und Texas.* Leipzig: Baumgartner, 1846. Eingehende Besprechung im *Deutschen Auswanderer,* SBAt LXVIII, 117.

Behr, Ottomar von. "Briefe über die Vereinscolonie." In supplement to the *Augsburger Allgemeine Zeitung,* October 3–5, 1846.

Bromme, Traugott. "Der Freistaat Texas." *Rathgeber für Auswanderungslustige. Wie und wohin sollen wir auswandern: nach den Vereinigten Staaten oder dem Freistaat Texas,* chap. 4. Stuttgart: Hoffmann, 1846.

Grund, Francis Joseph. *Handbuch und Wegweiser für Auswanderer nach den Vereinigten Staaten von Nord-Amerika und Texas.* 2nd. ed. Stuttgart and Tübingen: J. G. Cotta, 1846.

Kordül, A. *Der sicherer Führer nach und in Texas.* Rottweil am Neckar: J. P. Setzer, 1846.

Solms-Braunfels, Carl, Prinz von. *Texas, Geschildert in Beziehung auf seine geographischen, socialen und übrigen Verhältnissen mit besonderer Rücksicht auf die deutsche Colonisation.* Frankfurt am Main: Johann Davis Sauerländer, 1846.

Texas, ein Handbuch für deutsche Auswanderer mit besonderer Rücksicht auf diejenigen, welche ihre Überfahrt und Ansiedlung durch Hilfe des Vereins zum Schutze deutscher Einwanderer in Texas bewirken sollen. Official publication of the Association for the Protection of German Emigrants in Texas. Bremen, 1846.

1847

Anonymous. "Bericht eines unparteiischen Kaufmanns aus New Orleans über die Lage der Emigranten und von Meusebachs Tätigkeit." In *Die Weserzeitung*, n.d.

Behr, Ottomar von. *Guter Rath für Auswanderer nach den Vereinigten Staaten von Nord Amerika mit besonderer Berücksichtigung von Texas . . . nach eigner Erfahrung geschrieben.* Leipzig: Robert Friese, 1847.

Benner, A. "Briefe aus Texas . . . an Schlapp," Neu Braunfels, 24. In *Der Deutschen Auswanderer*, March 1847.

Bromme, Traugott. *Neustes vollständiges Hand- und Reisebuch für Auswanderer aus allen Klassen und jedem Stande nach den Vereinigten Staaten.* Bayreuth, 1847.

Büttner, Johann G. *Briefe aus und über Nordamerika.* Vol. 1. Dresden and Leipzig: Arnold, 1847.

Constant, L. Texas. *Das Verderben deutscher Auswanderer in Texas unter dem Schutze des Mainzer Verins.* Berlin: Reimer, 1847.

Fuchs, Adophus. "Briefe aus Texas." *Der deutsche Auswanderer*, no. 15, 1847.

Löher, Franz. *Geschichte und Zustände der Deutschen in Amerika.* Cincinnati: Eggers and Wulkop; Leipzig: K. F. Köhler, 1847.

Schütz, Baron von. *Texas. Rathgeber für Auswanderer.* Wiesbaden, 1847.

Sörgel, Alwin H. *Für Auswanderungslustige: Briefe eines unter dem Schutze des Mainzervereins nach Texas Ausgewanderten.* Leipzig, 1847. English-language version, *A Sojourn in Texas, 1846–1847*, translated and edited by W. M. Von-Maszewski. San Marcos: German Heritage Society, 1992.

Sommer, Karl von. *Bericht über meine Reise nach Texas im Jahre 1846.* Bremen, 1847.

1848

Behr, Ottomar von. *Die Vereinigten Staaten von Nordamerika.* Gotha: n.p., 1848.

Bromme, Traugott. "Der Staat Texas." In *Hand und Reisebuch für Auswanderer nach den Vereinigten Staaten von Nord-Amerika, Texas*, vol. 3. 5th ed. Bayreuth: Buchner, 1848.

1849

Bracht, Viktor. *Texas im Jahre 1848*. Elberfeld and Iserlohn: J. Bädeker, 1849.

Römer, Ferdinand von. *Texas: Mit besonderer Rücksicht auf deutsche Auswanderung und die physischen Verhältnisse des Landes nach eigener Beobachtung geschildert*. Bonn: Adolph Marcus, 1849.

1850

Bülow, v. "Instruktionen für die Auswanderer nach Texas durch ihn entworfen." 1850. In *Allgemeinen Auswanderungszeitung*, no. 3, January 7, 1851.

Herff, Ferdinand von. *Die geregelte Auswanderung des deutschen Proletariats mit besonderer Beziehung auf Texas*. Frankfurt am Main: Franz Varrentrapp, 1850.

Steinert, W. *Nordamerika, vorzüglich Texas im Jahre 1849*. Berlin: K.W. Krüger, 1850.

1851

Schlecht, Friedrich. *Mein Ausflug nach Texas*. Bunzlau: n.p., 1851.

1853

Bromme, Traugott. *Neustes vollständiges Hand- und Reisebuch für Auswanderer nach den Vereinigten Staaten von Nordamerika*. 7th ed., expanded and revised. Bamburg: Büttner, 1853.

Kapp, Friedrich. "Die Geschichte der deutschen Ansiedlungen des westlichen Texas und dessen Bedeutung für die Vereinigten Staaten." *Atlantischen Studien von Deutschen in Amerika* 1 (1853): 173 ff.

1855

Gerstäker, Friedrich. *Nach Amerika*. 1855.

Kapp, Frederick. "The History of Texas, Early German Colonization, Princes and Nobles in America: The Future of the State,
A Lecture by Frederick Kapp." *New York Daily Tribune*, January
20, 1855, p. 6, cols. 1–3.

Strubberg, Friedrich Armand. *Amerikanische Jagd- und Reiseabenteue
mit 24 von dem Verfasser selbst nach der Natur entworfenen Illustra-
tionen*, vol. 1. Stuttgart: J. G. Cotta, 1857.

1858

Fröbel, Julius. *Aus Amerika: Erfahrungen, Reisen und Studien.* 2 vols.
Leipzig: J. J. Weber, 1857–1858.

Strubberg, Friedrich Armand. *Bis in die Wildnis.* 5 vols. Breslau: Eduard Trewendt, 1858.

1859

Strubberg, Friedrich Armand. *An der Indianergrenze.* Hannover:
n.p., 1859.

—— *Alte und neue Heimath.* Breslau: Trewendt, 1859.

Strubberg, Friedrich Armand. *Szenen aus den Kämpfen der Mexikan-
er und Nordamerikaner.* Breslau: Eduard Trewendt, 1859.

1861

Strubberg, Friedrich Armand. *Schwarzes Blut oder: Sklaverei in
Amerika.* 3 vols. Hannover: Carl Rümpler, 1861.

1867

Strubberg, Friedrich Armand. *Friedrichsburg, die Colonie des
deutschen Fürsten-Vereins in Texas.* 2 vols. Leipzig: Friedrich
Fleischer, 1867.

1868

Strubberg, Friedrich Armand. *Aus Armands Frontierleben.* 2nd ed.
Hannover: n.p., 1868.

1872

Strubberg, Friedrich Armand. *Die Fürstentochter. Eine deutsche Gräfin wandert während der 1840er Jahre nach Texas aus.* 3 vols. Hannover, 1872.

Lightning Source UK Ltd.
Milton Keynes UK
UKHW040413291022
411179UK00012B/219